METCALFE
Card Construction Kits

🌐 metcalfemodels.com 📞 01729 830072 ✉ info@metcalfemodels.com

INDUSTRIAL

OLD MILL CHIMNEY STACK
00 SCALE - PO401 £9.00
N SCALE - PN991 £7.00

INDUSTRIAL OVERBRIDGE
00 SCALE - PO402 £8.50
N SCALE - PN992 £7.50

GRIMY OLD MILL
00 SCALE - PO290 £25.00
N SCALE - PN990 £18.00

Can be built as low relief building shown here, or a stand alone building.

RAMSHACKLE WORKSHOP
00 SCALE - PO286 £15.00
N SCALE - PN186 £12.00

OLD FACTORY
00 SCALE - PO287 £18.00
N SCALE - PN187 £14.00

BREWERY
00 SCALE - PO288 £19.00
N SCALE - PN188 £13.00

No 7 HIGH STREET SHOP FRONT
00 SCALE - PO374 £10.50
N SCALE - PN974 £9.00

TOWN BUILDINGS

HOTEL WEDNESDAY (LOW RELIEF)
00 SCALE - PO375 £16.50
N SCALE - PN975 £10.00

BUS STOP
00 SCALE - PO525 £6.50
00 SCALE ONLY

CINEMA & SHOPS (LOW RELIEF)
00 SCALE - PO206 £12.00
N SCALE - PN170 £8.50

PUB & SHOPS (LOW RELIEF)
00 SCALE - PO205 £15.00
N SCALE - PN972 £10.50

BANK & SHOP (LOW RELIEF)
00 SCALE - PO271 £13.50
N SCALE - PN971 £10.50

MARKET STALLS
00 SCALE - PO530 £6.50
N SCALE - PN830 £5.50

CASTLES

CASTLE HALL
00 SCALE - PO294 £19.50
N SCALE - PN194 £15.00

CASTLE WALL BRIDGE
00 SCALE - PO296 £11.00
N SCALE - PN196 £8.00

WATCH TOWER
00 SCALE - PO292 £7.00
N SCALE - PN192 £7.00

N Scale contains 2 Towers.

CASTLE GATEHOUSE
00 SCALE - PO291 £20.00
N SCALE - PN191 £16.00

CURTAIN WALLS
00 SCALE - PO293 £12.00 / N SCALE - PN193 £9.00

CATALOGUE
Call or e-mail us for a **FREE** catalogue.
📞 01729 830072 ✉ info@metcalfemodels.com

WEBSITE DOWNLOADS
Did you know you can download full scale footprints of our kits.
You can also print extra chimneys and curtains,
all from our website!

METCALFEMODELS.COM

f @metcalfemodels   𝕏 @metcalfekits   📷 metcalfemodelsandtoys

SKILLS GUIDE: CONTENTS

MODELLER'S GUIDE
LAYOUT CONSTRUCTION

ISBN: 978 1 80282 972 3
Editor: Mike Wild
Editorial team: Mark Chivers, Richard Foster
Senior editor, specials: Roger Mortimer
Email: roger.mortimer@keypublishing.com
Cover Design: Steve Donovan
Design: Steve Diggle and Panda Media
Advertising Sales Manager: Sam Clark
Email: sam.clark@keypublishing.com
Tel: 01780 755131
Advertising Production: Becky Antoniades
Email: Rebecca.antoniades@keypublishing.com

SUBSCRIPTION/MAIL ORDER
Key Publishing Ltd, PO Box 300,
Stamford, Lincs, PE9 1NA
Tel: 01780 480404
Subscriptions email: subs@keypublishing.com
Mail Order email: orders@keypublishing.com
Website: www.keypublishing.com/shop

PUBLISHING
Group CEO and Publisher: Adrian Cox

PUBLISHED BY
Key Publishing Ltd, PO Box 100,
Stamford, Lincs, PE9 1XQ
Tel: 01780 755131
Website: www.keypublishing.com

PRINTING
Precision Colour Printing Ltd, Haldane,
Halesfield 1, Telford, Shropshire. TF7 4QQ

DISTRIBUTION
Seymour Distribution Ltd,
2 Poultry Avenue, London, EC1A 9PU
Enquiries Line: 02074 294000.

We are unable to guarantee the bona fides of any of our advertisers. Readers are strongly recommended to take their own precautions before parting with any information or item of value, including, but not limited to money, manuscripts, photographs, or personal information in response to any advertisements within this publication.
© Key Publishing Ltd 2024
All rights reserved. No part of this magazine may be reproduced or transmitted in any form by any means, electronic or mechanical, including photocopying, recording or by any information storage and retrieval system, without prior permission in writing from the copyright owner. Multiple copying of the contents of the magazine without prior written approval is not permitted.

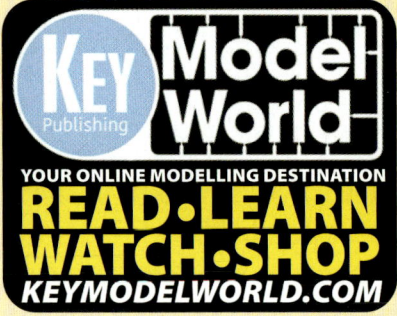

WHAT'S

8 Starting out
Mike Wild introduces the Skills Guide for layout construction.

10 In-tuition
Your introduction to the common scales and gauges in which to build a model railway.

14 Designing a railway
Choosing an era, finding a format and selecting a location - its all covered here.

20 DIY baseboards
We show you how to build your own baseboard using readily available tools and materials

24 Laser baseboards
We explore construction of a laser cut baseboard kit.

28 Building the GCR
The story behind development of this popular magazine layout.

38 Basic electrics
Top tips, advice and guidance on building a reliable and safe model railway.

44 Going digital
An introduction to the wonderful world of Digital Command Control.

50 Track planning
Learn how to design your layout and what to look out for along with inspirational examples.

56 A Fairlie Good Idea
A 'OO9' gauge in just 8ft x 2ft 6in modelling North Wales.

64 Track laying
A practical guide to the process of track laying.

70 Point motors
Discover how to operate your points hands-free.

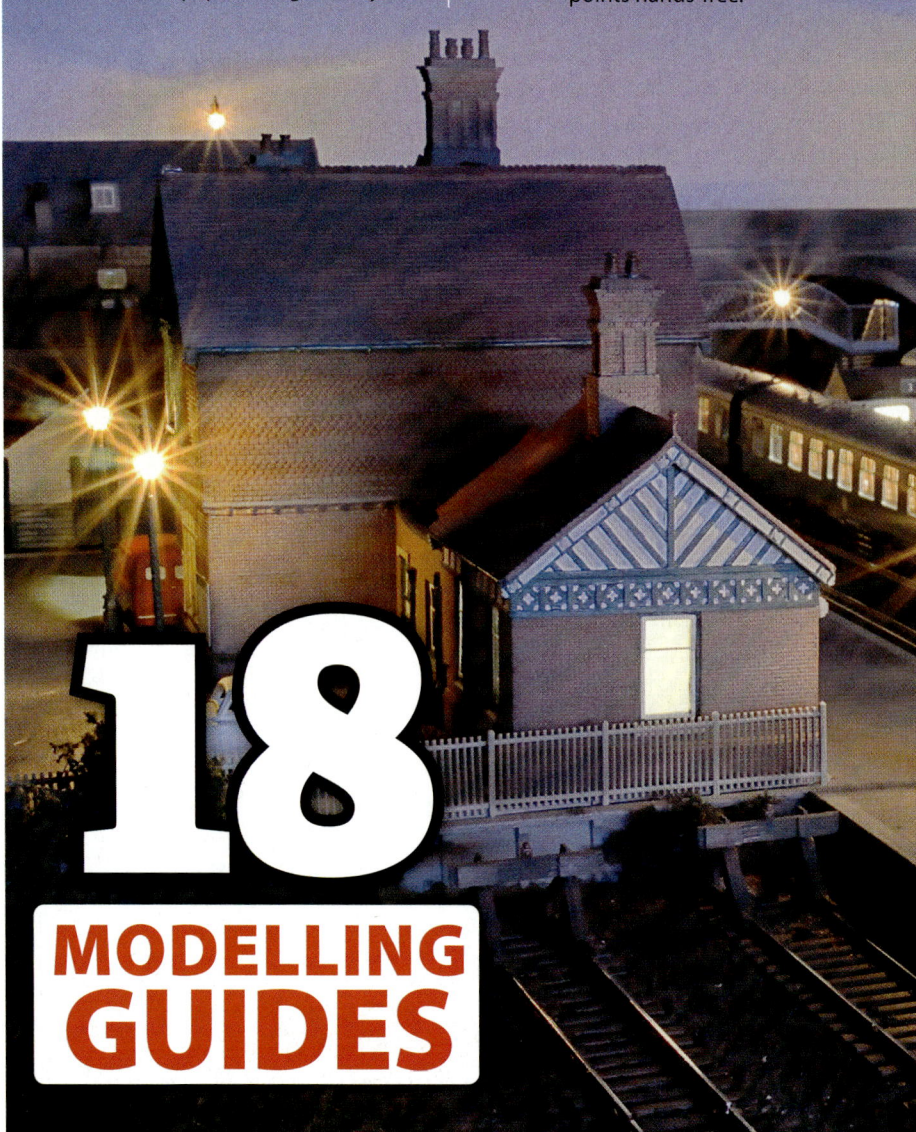

18 MODELLING GUIDES

INSIDE!

KEY SKILLS GUIDE
TRACK LAYING
- Techniques
- Tools
- Materials

74 Ballasting
We explain the simplicity behind realistic model ballast.

78 Platforms
Four methods for platform construction explained.

84 Semaphore signals
How to install Dapol semaphore signals for a realistic railway scene.

88 Add roads
Tips and techniques for simple ways to introduce roads to your railway scene.

92 Landscaping
How to create a landscape with cardboard and plaster cloth in simple steps.

96 Static grass
We show you how to make realistic grasses in miniature.

100 Simple trees
We show you how to make realistic trees quickly and with cost in mind and two differing methods.

104 Building in 'TT:120'
We explain the story behind Twelvemill Bridge - our new 'TT:120' scale layout.

112 Add lighting
How to use Woodland Scenics Just-Plug lighting accessories and system.

118 Detailing
Top tips for bringing life and detail to a model railway of any size and shape.

124 Maintenance
Keeping your completed layout in running order means regular maintenance. We explain all you need to know.

WE SHOW YOU HOW!

Hertfordshire's Leading Model Railway Specialist

 www.ks-models.co.uk

- ✓ All Major Manufacturers & More!
- ✓ N Gauge to O Gauge
- ✓ Tools, Paints & Materials
- ✓ Plastic Kits & Diecast
- ✓ Pre-owned
- ✓ Mail Order

30 Years in Stevenage
(44 years in business)

Email: russell@ks-models.co.uk

Shop:	Helpdesk:
01438 746616	**07858 546855**
Thurs - Sat, 10am - 5pm	Mon - Sat, 10am - 5pm
19 Middle Row, Stevenage SG1 3AW	Phone - Text - WhatsApp

Model Rail Baseboards

DREAM IT AND WE BUILD IT

Manufacturers of bespoke modular baseboard systems

Our baseboards are supplied fully assembled, the legs just simply bolt on.

Made from professional furniture grade MDF or Birch Ply the construction is open frame with a 9mm top making them light and incredibly strong and robust.

They are very stable and will not twist, warp or sag.

We custom make baseboards to order to meet your exact requirements.

We offer model railway clubs discount.

Gaming tables also available.

We offer a complete layout service.
We can design and build your layout from start to finish.
Track laying, electrical work, point control panels. ,Scenery.

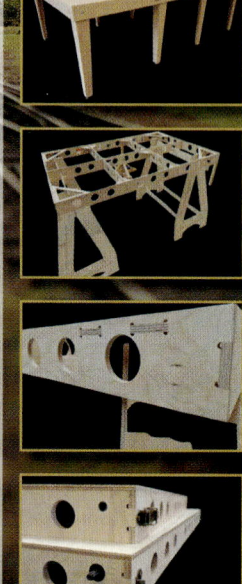

T: Ireland: **046 973 8858** UK: **0121 790 0468**
E: **sales@modelrailbaseboards.com**

www.modelrailbaseboards.com

Unit 1,
10-12 Alder Hills,
Poole, Dorset BH12 4AL

T: **01202 798068**

E: **info@modelrailwaysolutions.co.uk**

Est: 2010

www.modelrailwaysolutions.co.uk

COME VISIT OUR MODEL SHOP
We stock all well known brands and **FREE** parking
Open: 9.30am-5pm Mon-Fri
10am-4pm Saturdays

MODULAR BASEBOARDS
Hand-made in the UK, our baseboard products are popular worldwide.

WANTED
Railway items or collections

GIFT CARDS AVAILABLE

ONLINE SHOP
Visit our website and purchase one of many items.

BR/ELECTRO-MOTIVE DIESEL CLASS 66 LOCOMOTIVE

1:76.2 SCALE/OO GAUGE
DUE IN STOCK Q1 2024

accurascale

DC/DCC READY £169.99

DCC SOUND £259.99

All models shown are pre-production samples and are subject to refinement and alteration

SHED HEAVEN!

Accurascale have build the ultimate 'Shed' – the Class 66 in 1:76.2 scale. Our first colourful run consists of ten liveries including four special limited editions. The refined tooling suite enables a level of precision, finesse and detail that matches rest of our range. Future productions runs will ensure that our models will cover all the major and some of the more subtle variations of the class, over their successful 25 year career.

Both DC silent (DCC ready) and DCC sound versions are available for all our locomotives.

Scan the QR Code or visit: www.accurascale.com to view the full range of Class 66 locomotives available to order.

All Class 66 models feature

- High level of detail
- Die-cast chassis
- Five-pole motor with twin flywheels
- DCC ready & DCC sound (ESU loksound v5) options
- Details specific to individual prototypes
- High fidelity metal and plastic parts
- Rotating axle box hubs
- Helical gears for maximum performance

- Comprehensive lighting functions
- Enhancing the model with redesigned axle boxes for the smoothest running
- Easier decoder access with a lift off roof section upgrading the PCB to eliminate wiring
- Revised lighting to give access to day, night and yard mode under DCC
- Hall sensors added to DCC sound models

- Cab access step and handrails have been moved from body mount to chassis mount to allow for breakage free access to chassis
- Cab Front Handrails now have the option of 5 point or 7 point mounting with correct round profile handrail mounts
- And other typical Accurascale features.

www.accurascale.com

SKILLS GUIDE: LAYOUT CONSTRUCTION

Starting

WELCOME to the wonderful world of model railways. Your journey into this fascinating, enthralling and creative hobby begins here. It combines a rich tapestry of skills from designing and planning through carpentry and wiring to the ultimate creativity of modelling the real world in miniature.

The chances are, though, that you are here for the trains – and from that perspective you couldn't have picked a better time to start building a model railway. The support for product development and the availability of new locomotives, rolling stock and accessories is more buoyant than any time before. Plus, the standard of today's products – in everything from locomotives to accessories - means it is now simpler than ever to build your dream model railway. Add to this options for digital control and sound and we are now more able to get even closer to reality than ever before.

There are many reasons that you are likely to be reading this Skills Guide. You might be brand new to the world of modelmaking with no previous experience. You could be returning to the hobby like scores of others having had a break from modelling or you could already be in the process of building your layout and looking for advice and inspiration to take the next turn. You might have found an old collection in the loft and want to bring it back to life or it could be that you've seen the latest adverts for new products which sparked your imagination. Whichever reason it is, you are in the right place.

Model railway construction is at the very heart of what we do here at *Hornby Magazine*. It keeps us close to the hobby and helps us to fulfil the needs of modellers new and established. And we are proud to say that we really enjoy the challenge of building a new layout. All this means we are well versed in the skills required and we want to pass that information on to you.

out...

This Skills Guide from the team at Key Model World is a one-stop shop for all the information you need to get started in modelling. Consider the contents of these 132 pages a starting point as we show how to develop and improve your model railway in *Hornby Magazine* and online at Key Model World every month.

Here you can learn the basics: starting out with choosing the scale and era to suit you, we explain where you can locate a model railway and the positives and pitfalls of each, how to design your layout, provide examples of trackplans and, even more importantly, provide practical guides to the actual processes involved in making a layout of your own.

We've steered away from talking about locomotives and rolling stock directly here to keep the focus on layout construction. We explore building baseboards from scratch and with kits, explain the basics of model railway electrics, provide an introduction to digital control, reveal how to lay track for the best running, show you how to add realistic ballast, point motors, signals, roads, the basics of scenery, detail and even maintenance.

Added to this we have also profiled three of the layouts built by the team – all of which have a story to tell. Significantly, all three follow the line 'a model railway is never finished' as each has been dramatically modified from its original creation as our ideas, space and designs have grown. That is all part of the fun – developing a model railway from its original concept and taking it further than you ever imagined you could!

We hope you enjoy this Skills Guide on Layout Construction and that it inspires your project and its development. Let us know what you are building by writing to *hornbymagazine@keypublishing.com* - we really enjoy seeing modellers' creations at any stage of their lifetime.

Happy modelling!

Mike Wild
Editor, *Hornby Magazine.*

Building a scenic model railway is a brilliant experience, taking it through from concept to creation to capture a small slice of the world in miniature. This 'OO' gauge layout is called Shortley Bridge. A Bachmann 'WD' 2-8-0 is about to depart from this country station with goods train while the goods yard on the left bustles with activity. In this Skills Guide, we will arm you with the basics to be able create scenes like this.
Mike Wild/Hornby Magazine.

SKILLS GUIDE: LAYOUT CONSTRUCTION

SCALES

Gauging interest

What size model trains shoudl I use? That choice used to be quite limited but today we have five main options to choose from... **MIKE WILD** takes a closer look.

NOT SO LONG AGO we were faced with only two choices when it came to building a model railway with ready-to-run rolling stock – 'OO' and 'N' gauges. Offering models in 4mm:1ft and 2mm:1ft scale, 'OO' and 'N' were well supported with locomotives, carriages, wagons from major manufacturers while an array of smaller suppliers produced everything from buildings down to the smallest street details.

Today though the choice has doubled. 'OO' gauge is still king when it comes to availability and popularity, but alongside 'N' gauge, it has been joined by an increasing portfolio of ready-to-run products for 'O' gauge (7mm:1ft scale) while new kid on the block is 'TT:120'. And if you like narrow gauge railways, Bachmann, Heljan and Peco now offer a range of 'OO9' narrow gauge models from Bachmann, Heljan and Peco.

There are many other choices beyond the main four, but 'OO', 'N', 'O' and 'OO9' are the most accessible for all. Alternatives include finescale versions of 'OO' gauge – 'EM' and 'P4' which use 18.2mm and 18.83mm gauge track respectively – while there is also a finescale equivalent of 'N' gauge in 2mm scale which uses 9.42mm gauge track. You will also find reference to 'HO' scale for European outline models, as well as specialist British outline products, which are produced to 3.5mm:1ft. Overseas modellers also have access to a wider range of narrow gauge tracks and models including 'HOe' (the same as 'OO9' using 9mm gauge track) and 'HOm' which is used to represent metre-gauge lines using 12mm gauge track. Europe also still models extensively in 3mm:1ft scale, 'TT', using locomotives and rolling stock running on 12mm gauge track, a gauge which lost its place in the British ready-to-run market in the mid-1960s.

There is an extensive choice and we have listed all the readily available popular scales and gauges in Table 1, but for now we will concentrate on the 'big four'…

'OO' GAUGE
- **Track gauge:** 16.5mm
- **Scale:** 4mm:1ft
- **Association:** www.doubleogauge.com

'OO' gauge has its origins in the 1920s when Bing introduced its first clockwork models to 16.5mm gauge and scaled to 4mm:1ft. However, it really took off from 1938 when Meccano launched its Hornby Dublo range and the scale and gauge combination has dominated British outline modelling ever since.

Today, 'OO' gauge is by far the best supported and most popular of all the model railway scales in Britain. Locomotives, carriages and wagons are readily available as out of the box products and a constant stream of new releases are delivered on a regular basis from big names including Bachmann, Dapol, Heljan and Hornby. In recent years these have been joined by an increasing number of ready-to-run manufacturers including Accurascale, Rapido Trains, Revolution Trains and Oxford Rail. Retailers including Kernow Model Rail Centre, Rails of Sheffield and The Model Centre have produced or commissioned exclusive models, further extending the range.

Beyond ready-to-run, there is an extensive array of kit manufacturers producing models in injection moulded plastic, resin, white metal and brass. Combined, they offer something to suit every railway situation and suiting a range of skill levels from beginner to advanced.

However, it isn't just rolling stock which keeps 'OO' gauge going. There are large ranges of ready made buildings from Bachmann

Right: Narrow gauge modelling is set to take flight in ready-to-run with the arrival of new models from Bachmann, Heljan and Peco. However, until now it has been the preserve of kit and scratch building for an accurate scene. This is Charles Insley's Maesog modelling Welsh slate railway operations in 'OO9'.

Scenecraft and Hornby Skaledale while Oxford has introduced a new Oxford Structures section to its portfolio. There is also a huge diversity of kits available for buildings and structures while many overseas 'HO' scale buildings will look perfectly at home on a 'OO' gauge model railway too.

Figures, lineside details, road vehicles, lighting, signals, level crossings and every other accessory you can think of are available. A quick internet search or visit to your local model shop will soon present you with an extensive range of product choices - whether you are looking for a new locomotive or just a simple sign to finish off a station scene.

Track, a bone of contention as 16.5mm gauge track doesn't represent an accurate gauge for 4mm:1ft scale models, is readily available with a choice of Code 100 and Code 75 flat bottom rail and, more recently, the addition of bullhead rail track and points from Peco which are ready to lay. C&L Finescale, DCC Concepts and others producing scale sleeper 16.5mm gauge track.

So long as you can live with the track gauge compromise – and the vast majority accept this quite readily, 'OO' gauge is usually the first choice for a new modeller because it has so much support in both modelling communities and products. »

MANUFACTURER LINKS

BRAND	SCALES	WEBSITE
Bachmann (Branchline/Graham Farish/ Narrow Gauge/EFE	'OO', 'N', 'OO9'	www.bachmann.co.uk
Dapol (inc. Lionheart Trains)	'OO', 'N', 'O' and O-16.5'	www.dapol.co.uk
Hornby	'OO'	www.hornby.com
Heljan	'OO', 'OO9' and 'O'	www.heljan.dk
Rapido Trains	'N' and 'OO'	www.rapidotrains.co.uk
Revolution Trains (plus Sonic Models)	'N' and 'OO'	www.revolutiontrains.com
Accurascale	'OO'	https://www.accurascale.com/
Oxford Rail	'OO'	www.oxfordrail.com
Peco/Ratio/Wills/Parkside Models	'OO', 'N', 'OO9' and 'O'	www.peco-uk.com
Clark Railworks	'OO' and 'O'	www.clarkrailworks.com
Minerva Model Railways	'O'	www.minervamodelrailways.co.uk
KR Models	'OO'	www.krmodels.net
Kernow Model Rail Centre	'OO'	www.kernowmodelrailcentre.com
Rails of Sheffield	'OO' and 'N'	www.railsofsheffield.com
Cavalex	'OO'	www.cavalexmodels.com
The Model Centre (TMC)	'OO'	www.themodelcentre.com
Planet Industrials	'OO'	www.planetindustrials.co.uk
Olivia's Trains	'OO'	www.oliviastrains.com

'OO' gauge is the most popular scale in British modelling – it has an incredible variety of locomotives and rolling stock as well as all manner of accessories. A Heljan 'Western' hydraulic stands in the stabling siding next to a roundhouse assembled from ready made Kernow Model Rail Centre buildings which house a Bachmann '57XX' 0-6-0PT, Collett '2251' 0-6-0, Hornby '2884' 2-8-0 and a Heljan 'Hymek' in the distance.

SKILLS GUIDE: LAYOUT CONSTRUCTION

SCALES

'N' GAUGE
- **Track gauge:** 9mm
- **Scale:** 2mm:1ft
- **Association:** www.ngaugesociety.com

'N' gauge took off in the 1960s and offers a scale which requires a quarter of the space of 'OO' gauge and is modelled at 2mm:1ft scale. British outline rolling stock is made to 1:148 scale and runs on 9mm gauge track which is available in Code 80 and Code 55 rail profiles – the lower the number, the finer the rail.

The scale has great support from the N Gauge Society, established in 1967, and in the past decade has seen great advances in the standard of detail and performance that its models are capable of. Two manufacturers lead the charge in ready-to-run – Graham Farish as part of the Bachmann portfolio and Dapol, ably supported by the likes of Revolution Trains, Rapido Trains and EFE. The N Gauge Society has been prolific in supporting the scale, first with its own range of exclusive wagon kits but more recently in commissioning its own series of ready-to-run models through Dapol and Graham Farish.

Like 'OO' gauge there is an extensive range of suppliers for buildings, structures and detailing components while a number of manufacturers also develop kits in a variety of materials to allow more unusual items of rolling stock to be built.

What was once the underdog is now a viable alternative to 'OO' gauge for the space-restricted modeller. For example, a main line scene with scale length trains can, with some compromises, be built in as little as 6ft x 2ft while if you have more space the grandeur of a railway in the landscape is perfectly possible without the need to buy a barn. There are a great number of high profile 'N' gauge exhibition layouts on the circuit and this scale is well worth investigating as it continues to develop.

'O' GAUGE
- **Track gauge:** 32mm
- **Scale:** 7mm:1ft
- **Association:** www.gauge0guild.com

'O' gauge has been around since the earliest days of clockwork model railways. The ready-to-run revolution started in 2005 when Heljan released its Class 35 'Hymek'. Since then, the Danish firm has releaed an impressive number of ready-to-run diesel locomotives together with carriages and wagons.

However, it is the introduction to 'O' gauge of Dapol, Minerva and Clark Railworks which have really set the wheels in motion for the growth in the scale's popularity with ready-to-

GAUGE OR SCALE?
What's the difference between 'gauge' and 'scale'?
Gauge refers to the distance between the rails, which is usually measured in millimetres.
Scale is how to describe how many times smaller a model is to its real-life counterpart. This is usually expressed as a ratio (for example, 'OO' is 1:76 and 'N' is 1:148) or as 'millimetres to the foot' so that something that's 1ft long in reality is only 4mm long in 'OO' or 2mm long in 'N'.

A Class 56 draws into West Riding Power Station on *Hornby Magazine's* 1980s set exhibition model built in 'N' gauge. The Dapol model is dwarfed by the Bachmann Scenecraft cooling towers, a scene which would be difficult to replicate in 'OO' gauge on space grounds.

run modellers. Products have become readily available and at affordable prices.

Detail is key in 7mm scale and again there is a wide range of suppliers producing everything from nameplates to transfers, lineside details, track, buildings, road vehicles and more. Peco produces a range of ready made track and points with code 124 bullhead rail and this now includes curves for second radius set track making a simple circuit an easier prospect than before.

The only downside is the amount of space that 'O' requires. A basic circuit of Peco second radius track will require at least 9ft x 9ft to allow it to be joined together. That said, 'O' is perfect for compact shunting layouts. These can be built in 8ft or less but the larger scale enables much more detail to be included than some of the smaller ones.

Tthere is something really quite special about 'O' gauge and its imposing locomotives and rolling stock and, as the range of products continues to increase, it becomes ever more enticing and popular.

Z It's worth noting here that Dapol's sister company Lionheart Trains has produced the first 'O-16.5' narrow gauge models - that is 7mm:1ft scale trains running on 'OO' track. The initial range comprises Lynton & Barnstaple locomotives and stock, while Dapol has used the Kitmaster brand to produce a range of L&B building kits in this scale.

'OO9' GAUGE
- **Track gauge:** 9mm
- **Scale:** 4mm:1ft
- **Assoication:** www.009society.com

'OO9' isn't new to British outline modelling, but it is in the world of ready-to-run products. It started with Peco's ready-to-run carriages and wagons for the scale alongside Heljan's Lynton & Barnstaple Railway locomotives.
Peco has since joined forces with Kato to produce ready-to-run 'OO9' locomotives.

Bachmann has embraced 'OO9'. Its Narrow Gauge range includes Baldwin 4-6-0Ts, 'Quarry Hunslets', FR 'Double Fairlies', Baguley diesels, slate wagons and Ashover Light Railway carriages to name but a few.

Happily, being modelled to 4mm:1ft scale, all the accessories available for 'OO' gauge including buildings, road vehicles, people, animals and lineside fixtures are all well suited to a narrow gauge scene in 'OO9'.

As things stand 'OO9' looks set for a big boost with the arrival of the new locomotives from Bachmann and Heljan while these are already supported by an extensive range of narrow gauge track products from Peco. Plus, if you look a little further, Roco and Minitrains – available through Gaugemaster – produce collections of overseas prototype rolling stock, much of which can be used on British outline narrow gauge layouts too. The Bachmann Scenecraft range includes a collection of ready made resin buildings which take inspiration from the Lynton & Barnstaple Railway and there are sure to be more in the future. It's all making 'OO9' much more available to the masses.

WHAT IS CODE?
Model railway track is described in 'Code'. It refers to the rail height – 80 being 80 thousandths of an inch and 55 being 55 thousandths of an inch.

SCALES

TABLE 1 – POPULAR SCALES AND GAUGES

NAME	SCALE	RATIO	TRACK GAUGE	OUTLINE	ASSOCIATION	NOTES
'OO'	4mm:1ft	1:76	16.5mm	British	www.doubleogauge.com	Standard gauge
'EM'	4mm:1ft	1:76	18.2mm	British	www.emgs.org	Standard gauge
'P4'	4mm:1ft	1:76	18.83mm	British	www.scalefour.org	Standard gauge
'OO9'/'HOe'	4mm:1ft	1:76	9mm	British and overseas	www.009society.com	Narrow gauge
'N'	2mm:1ft	1:148	9mm	British and overseas	www.ngaugesociety.com	Standard gauge
2mm FS	2mm:1ft	1:148	9.42mm	British	www.2mm.org.uk	Standard gauge
'O'	7mm:1ft	1:43.5	32mm	British and overseas	www.gauge0guild.com	Standard gauge
Scale 7	7mm:1ft	1:43.5	33mm	British	www.scaleseven.org.uk	Standard gauge
O-16.5	7mm:1ft	1:43.5	16.5mm	British	www.7mmnga.org.uk	Narrow gauge
'HO'	3.5mm:1ft	1:87	16.5mm	Overseas/British	www.british-ho.com	Standard gauge
'TT'	3mm:1ft	1:102	12mm	Overseas/British	www.3smr.co.uk	Standard gauge
Gauge 1	10mm:1ft	1:32	44.45mm	British	www.g1mra.com	Standard gauge

'TT:120' GAUGE

l Track gauge: 12mm
l Scale: 2.54mm:1ft
l Association: uk.hornby.com/community/hornbytt120-club

2022 brought a brand-new and unchartered scale to the British market – 'TT:120'. This new addition has been spearheaded by Hornby but Peco, Gaugemaster and others are producing complementary rolling stock and accessories. new names have entered to the 'TT:120' fold making it more exciting than ever to consider a model railway in this new scale.

'TT:120' has long been part of the European modelling scene, but has never before been available to the British market. In the 1960s Tri-ang dabbled with British outline 'TT' to 3mm scale, but still using 12mm gauge track, and like all British scales was a compromise between scale and gauge – the scale being larger than the track gauge.

The new 'TT:120' products are the first true scale models for the British market where no matter which component you buy for your layout, they are matched in scale with the correct gauge of track to match the trains. The 1:120 scale works out at 2.54mm:1ft with one of its biggest advantages being that a much larger amount of railway can be fitted into a smaller space, but it is also larger than the already established 'N' gauge product range.

As you might expect the initial development of 'TT:120' was limited to a small group of products, but over its first year of availability the range has grown rapidly with much more to come, making it an ideal time to start construction of a new layout.

As they say, the choice is yours and, as we will explain in the following pages, choosing the scale is just one step towards building your dream model railway. ∎

'O' gauge is gaining ground at present with the regular release and announcement of new locomotives, carriages and wagons – the only downside is it needs more space than any of the other scales discussed here. A Heljan Class 37/0, modified, repainted and detailed, arrives at Wick End – an 18ft long Scottish Region terminus built by Chris and Dave Warner.

SKILLS GUIDE: LAYOUT CONSTRUCTION

Designing a model railway

Designing your layout requires more than simply building the baseboards and laying track. **MARK CHIVERS** explains the process from choosing a scale and era through to finding a location to build your dream railway.

DECISIONS, decisions, decisions. You will quickly come to realise that before you can lay a single piece of track that you need to give much thought to a combination of factors such as the type of layout you'd like to build, the era you want to depict, the gauge or scale and, most importantly, where to house it.

Layouts can be designed in all manner of shapes and sizes from simple continuous loops to figure-of-eight and multiple loop combinations, as well as end-to-end station and yard schemes in straight, 'L' shaped or 'U' shaped configurations. Will it be a simple out and back scheme or perhaps a through station with storage yard to storage yard operation? Factor in multiple-level layout designs and before you know it you are going to need quite a large space to house the finished article. If space is a major issue, don't worry for building a micro-layout, small shunting plank or depot scene to fill a corner can be just as satisfying as something larger.

Scale & gauge

As we've already established, there are plenty of size options to choose from when considering your layout design with 'N', 'OO9', 'OO' and 'O' – and now 'TT:120' – gauges amongst the most popular. An 'O' gauge layout will require considerably more space than its 'N' gauge equivalent, and the smaller scale will allow more scope for adding extra trackwork, buildings and features, which is ideal if you have limited space in which to house your new creation. However, it is also worth considering the 'less is more' mantra too, in which case 'O' gauge may be just the ticket for your modelling skills, by taking a less extensive, but more detailed, approach.

Interest in 'O' gauge modelling has been steadily on the rise, due in part to the availability of ready-to-run locomotives and rolling stock from the likes of Dapol, Heljan and Minerva Models together with a supporting cast of kits and growing selection of accessories and ready-built structures.

'OO' gauge, as outlined in our guide to scales and gauges, is by far the most popular and traditional choice, with a seemingly endless supply of products and scenic accessories, which also helps when it comes to decision making. 'OO9' or 'TT:120' modelling may also offer an interesting alternative, given recent ready-to-run introductions from Bachmann, Heljan, Hornby and Peco. Some quite involved designs could be developed in a small space in both scales.

Era

Next, you will need to think about the period you wish to model. Some of the major manufacturers including Bachmann and Hornby use an era system to define specific periods of railway history which incorporates pre-Grouping, the Big Four era, British Railways (early and late periods), BR pre-TOPs, BR TOPS, BR sectorisation, privatisation and the contemporary scene. Each era is defined by years, with overlap between periods, where appropriate. This system really comes into its own when choosing appropriate rolling stock for motive power, enabling matching passenger and goods trains to be assembled easily. 'OO' and 'N' gauges are certainly well represented in terms of available motive power and rolling stock through the eras, together with extensive ranges of accessories and ready-made cast resin buildings and laser-cut kits to help populate a layout.

Selecting an era is really a personal choice. We all have our own preferences – multiples in some cases – but often layout design is swayed by memories of the past or recent adventures on the real railway. This will also be affected by the area of the country you want to model – Scottish Highlands are very different in their terrain to the Southern Region of BR, but even within regions the terrain and railway style have great variety.

Chances are you already have an idea of the area and period you want to model, but research through pictorial books will provide a world of photographic information to inspire your project.

Format

Once you have agreed on the scale and era to be modelled, you can now decide on the type of layout you'd like to build. If you have grand designs on a large multi-platform station arrangement, with a locomotive depot, carriage sidings, goods yard and a series of fast and slow continuous loop lines, clearly you will need plenty of space to allow your scheme to breathe.

'N' gauge may be worth considering, if the space you have available is limited, although with a little creativity you may find that you can still model your scheme in 'OO' gauge by tweaking the design and making the area work for you.

If a large continuous loop layout is not possible, you may wish to consider an 'L' shaped end-to-end scheme that runs along two walls, or 'U' shape design across three walls. These styles of »

DESIGNING A LAYOUT

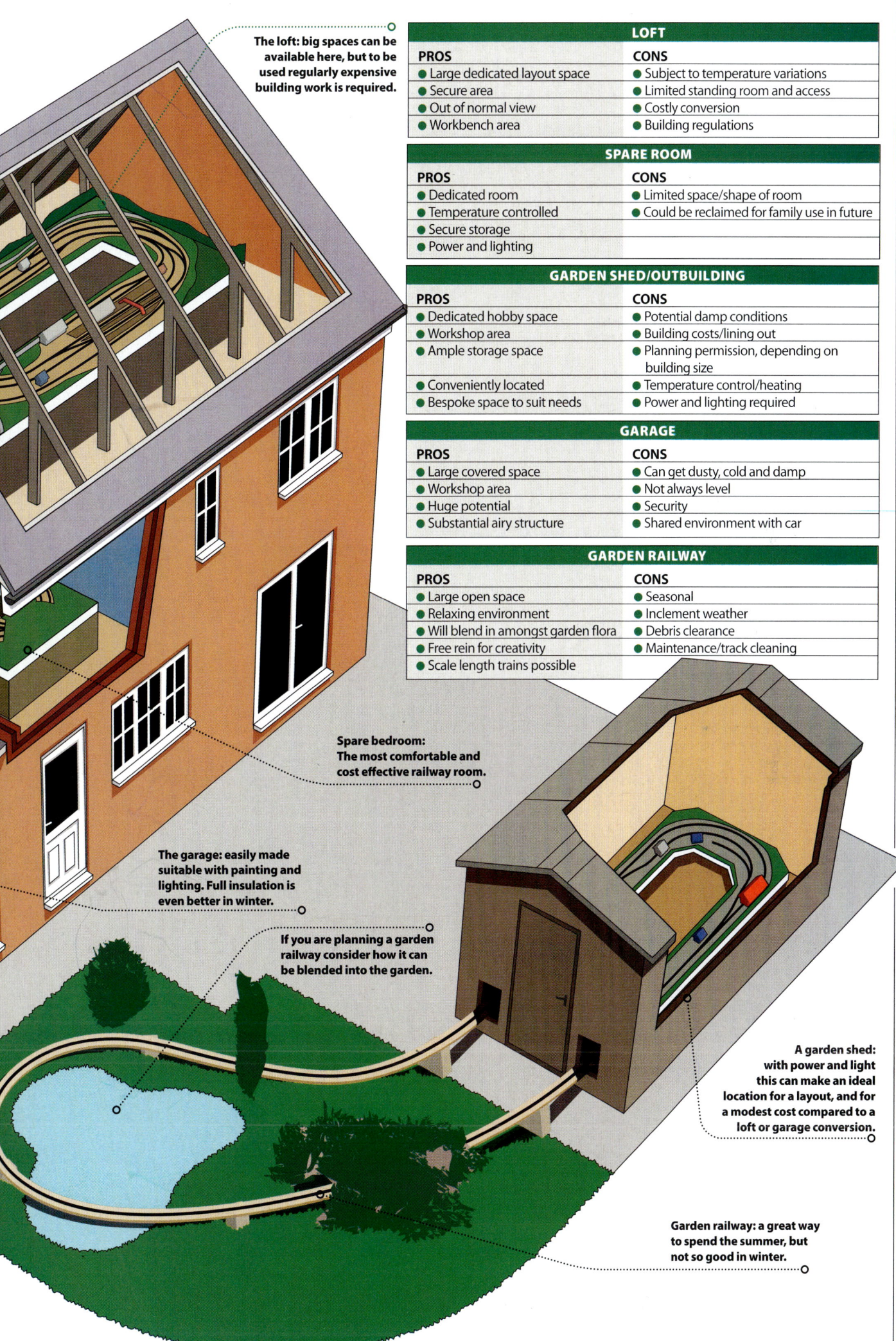

LOFT

PROS	CONS
• Large dedicated layout space	• Subject to temperature variations
• Secure area	• Limited standing room and access
• Out of normal view	• Costly conversion
• Workbench area	• Building regulations

SPARE ROOM

PROS	CONS
• Dedicated room	• Limited space/shape of room
• Temperature controlled	• Could be reclaimed for family use in future
• Secure storage	
• Power and lighting	

GARDEN SHED/OUTBUILDING

PROS	CONS
• Dedicated hobby space	• Potential damp conditions
• Workshop area	• Building costs/lining out
• Ample storage space	• Planning permission, depending on building size
• Conveniently located	• Temperature control/heating
• Bespoke space to suit needs	• Power and lighting required

GARAGE

PROS	CONS
• Large covered space	• Can get dusty, cold and damp
• Workshop area	• Not always level
• Huge potential	• Security
• Substantial airy structure	• Shared environment with car

GARDEN RAILWAY

PROS	CONS
• Large open space	• Seasonal
• Relaxing environment	• Inclement weather
• Will blend in amongst garden flora	• Debris clearance
• Free rein for creativity	• Maintenance/track cleaning
• Scale length trains possible	

The loft: big spaces can be available here, but to be used regularly expensive building work is required.

Spare bedroom: The most comfortable and cost effective railway room.

The garage: easily made suitable with painting and lighting. Full insulation is even better in winter.

If you are planning a garden railway consider how it can be blended into the garden.

A garden shed: with power and light this can make an ideal location for a layout, and for a modest cost compared to a loft or garage conversion.

Garden railway: a great way to spend the summer, but not so good in winter.

SKILLS GUIDE: LAYOUT CONSTRUCTION

DESIGNING A LAYOUT

layout can still be exciting and engaging if you factor in plenty of operational interest.

You might opt for a large terminus station and goods yard at one end, while incorporating a small industrial concern at the other, or even a smaller station halt together with some off-scene storage. Perhaps a traditional country branch line terminus scene may be more in keeping with the space available. Alternatively, you may opt to model a busy locomotive depot or freight yard, with a constant stream of traffic fed from the off-scene storage area.

This design stage is the time to unleash your imagination. Equally, a small micro-layout with enough space to shunt a few wagons in a yard may suffice or even provide a test bed to learn new skills in track laying, electrics and scenic development. With the latter you could develop a shunting sequence to help keep the layout exciting to operate.

In a spare room an 'L' or 'U' shaped layout can be built around the walls where it is perfectly possible to recreate realistic branch line operations in 'OO' gauge. This is Axe Regis, a 7ft 6in x 2ft Southern Region branch line terminus created by the *Hornby Magazine* team.
Mike Wild/*Hornby Magazine*.

Location

You may already have noticed a common thread – space. Where do you house your new layout? Once you have an indicator of the size and scale of your layout, you can then assess the options in terms of where to build it. A spare room within the house is often preferable, as it provides a secure and temperature-controlled environment to work on and store your layout, as well as the motive power, rolling stock, buildings and accessories. It is also often the most cost-effective option, with fewer associated startup costs.

In an ideal world, the room would be a straightforward box-shape enabling you to build the layout using uniform-sized baseboards around the edge. However, in the real world, this isn't always the case as wardrobes, alcoves, doorways and more, seemingly conspire to make the job that little bit more difficult. It could be that you don't have a room spare, but there may be space in a bedroom or living space for an 'L' shaped or 'U' shaped layout along the walls, perhaps located above chests of drawers or cupboards, making good use of the available space.

Another alternative within the house is to be a form of portable layout which can be stored when not in use and assembled promptly when required. Typically a railway of this nature would either be on a single board, such as a traditional 6ft x 4ft train set style, or on a small group of smaller boards which can be accessed and bolted together quickly and simply. As you will see on pages 24-27, there are now laser cut baseboard options which take all the hassle out of building boards. With alignment dowels assembly of a pair of baseboards can be as quick as a few minutes. It's all in the planning and design.

Lofty ideas

An alternative is the loft area, which could be ideal for housing a layout, although it may require a considerable amount of conversion work before it is suitable to use. Given this space houses beams that are fundamental to the structural integrity of your house, you should always seek professional advice before embarking on any work or conversion of the loft area.

Not all lofts are suitable, but if the space can be professionally converted, it will transform the area and open up a useable space in which to house a layout. This area of space would enable a large scheme to be built with all manner of features included too, such as extra loops, hidden storage areas, tunnels, multiple stations, depots, goods yards, scenic vistas and more. You may even find a workbench could also be accommodated.

Whilst a professional conversion should include it, bear in mind that the loft will require insulating and lining to mitigate against extremes of temperature, while floorboards will need installing between the joists as well as extra timbers to support the roof, electrics and lighting too. It is also important to make sure you can stand upright whilst constructing and operating the layout, otherwise you may find it becomes a chore every time you head to the loft. Access, too, can be problematic, as it is often via a ladder, unless you can incorporate this into the overall conversion project.

Garage solution

If indoors is a problem, the garage offers a sheltered outdoor alternative. It may be part of the house with direct access or separate with an access door in addition to the usual large opening door/doors. Typically, single garages can measure anywhere between 16ft x 8ft to 20ft x 10ft while a double garage may offer up to a 20ft x 20ft space – each scenario ideal for hosting a model railway layout. What's more, they are usually effectively rectangular boxes, which certainly helps when it comes to baseboard construction and mounting.

Often, modern garages feature a power supply and light socket, which is a bonus – although these may need upgrading, while older structures may require the attention of a professional electrician before you can get things up and running. However, once you have the space available, you can build an impressive model railway in the space available.

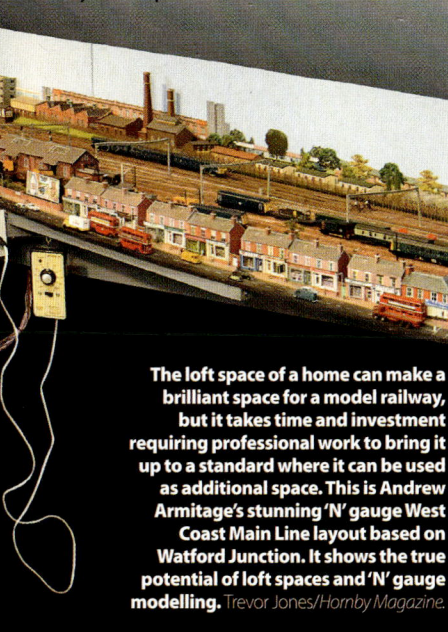

The loft space of a home can make a brilliant space for a model railway, but it takes time and investment requiring professional work to bring it up to a standard where it can be used as additional space. This is Andrew Armitage's stunning 'N' gauge West Coast Main Line layout based on Watford Junction. It shows the true potential of loft spaces and 'N' gauge modelling. *Trevor Jones/Hornby Magazine.*

Where space is limited, and the ideal project for the budding locomotive collector, a depot scene is a good choice. With the potential to build a detailed and working scene in 6ft x 2ft a depot provides great potential for learning new skills. *Mike Wild/Hornby Magazine.*

If you still require the garage for its original purpose, the layout could be attached to a pulley system to allow it to be stored out of the way while a car is parked within. Of course, not all layouts need to be large, and a smaller scheme might be accommodated at one end of the garage, clear of the car.

Whilst the garage may feature a modicum of lining in the roof space, it will still be subject to extremes of temperature and possibly damp conditions, so would no doubt benefit from some insulation/lining and a heat source to keep you warm whilst operating the layout through the autumn and winter. You may also wish to add draught excluders to the large garage doors.

ERA SYSTEM		
ERA	DESCRIPTION	YEARS
1	Pioneering	1804-1869
2	Pre-Grouping	1870-1922
3	Grouping	1923-1947
4	Early British Railways	1948-1956
5	Late British Railways	1957-1968
6	British Rail pre-TOPS	1957-1971
7	British Rail TOPS	1971-1986
8	BR Sectorisation	1982-1997
9	Privatisation	1996-2008
10	Network Franchising	2006-2017
11	Present Day	2014-on

Outdoor options

Alternative outdoor solutions include off-the-shelf or bespoke wooden/metal garden sheds and perhaps even brick buildings designed specifically for your model railway requirements. Whilst the former may be available ready-to-build, the latter will usually require professional design work and, if above a certain size, planning permission may be required.

Sheds and outdoor buildings in general offer an ideal environment for building layouts and pursuing the hobby, with workshop/workbench space as well. Clearly, there are costs associated with having a bespoke building, ranging from levelling of the ground in preparation for the structure, through to electrics and heating arrangements within the finished building, but the resulting hobby space will be worth it.

Given the UK weather patterns, it is advisable to insulate and line the shed interior and source adequate heating to maintain a consistent temperature that will protect the layout and associated stock from potentially damp or extreme conditions. Security could also be an issue, so it is worth considering your options such as window bars, a heavy-duty lock and alarm system.

Staying outdoors, you could also develop a garden layout. Suited to 'OO' gauge applications and above, rails can be incorporated within the »

The garden holds great potential for a model railway, especially where space is available for a shed building. Installing a shed requires ground to be levelled, a concrete or slab base and assembly of the building including insulation, power and lighting. The results speak for themselves in Philip Goodwin's Acol Pier (HM118) which uses the full length of the shed together with an additional outside running line for the return curve. *Trevor Jones/Hornby Magazine.*

SKILLS GUIDE: LAYOUT CONSTRUCTION

DESIGNING A LAYOUT

general layout of the garden running along specially built track bases amongst flower beds, plants, water features, rockeries and more. What better way to relax and watch your trains run by?

While care will be needed in wiring the layout track sections and any accessories, the outcome will reap benefits especially with scale-length train formations possible, thanks to the extra space an outdoor layout affords. Tunnels and bridges can be developed using suitable outdoor materials, while off-the-shelf resin cast models, such as those in Bachmann's Scenecraft and Hornby's Skaledale ranges, could be utilised. These are remarkably resilient outdoors, especially when treated with a sealing varnish over the factory paint finish.

You could also combine an outdoor layout with a shed, which would also offer somewhere to store the stock when not in use. The shed could house the main station complex and depots, while the garden layout hosts a few smaller calling points and yards along the way.

Garden layouts are, by their nature, seasonal and do require a high degree of maintenance ahead of any running sessions, due to the weather, plant detritus and animal/insect activity.

Track will need a rigorous cleaning regime to ensure electrical continuity, while any tunnels and bridges will require clearance of any obstructions before trains can run. It will also be necessary to ensure all track connections are still as they should be, especially on warm days when the sun can cause expansion issues. Also, consider carefully the track you are planning to use outdoors – the more delicate it is, the more chance there is of it distorting in direct sunlight or extreme cold.

A sizeable question

Having identified potential locations for your layout, the next task is to decide on the overall dimensions of your layout and whether it is to be a permanent or mobile structure. Are you planning to build it in place and leave it there, or will it be easily dismantled? Can it fill a whole room permanently, or does it need space around the edges? These factors will determine how the layout is secured and stored within a room.

Where space is at a premium in the home a compact shunting layout can provide the solution. With careful track planning an interesting layout can be built with plenty of operational potential. This is Paul Marshall-Potter's Shelfie which measures just over 4ft x 1ft for the scenic area with an additional 2ft long off scene storage plank. *Mike Wild/Hornby Magazine.*

Baseboard size is important, particularly if there's a chance you may need to transport it in the future. You may decide on conventional 4ft x 2ft boards amalgamated to create an 8ft x 4ft layout space in the centre of the room or perhaps utilise each individual board along one wall, or around the entire room – there are many permutations and the choice is yours. Boards over 4ft long can be cumbersome when moving or transporting them, while equally any board over 3ft wide will also prove difficult to reach across in a permanent layout situation.

At this design stage, also think about the additional features you may wish to incorporate. Will all track be on plain baseboards, or are you intending to add scenic structures such as viaducts or bridges or multi-level scenery? If so, you may need to build some open baseboards, which allows you to add extra visual interest to the overall design.

For something a little more involved, you may wish to include a multi-level baseboard design, with the upper board appearing fully scenic, while the lower example may feature storage lines and plain track, with a helix track formation at each end to enable trains to rise and fall to the relevant baseboards.

A garage can be a very useable space for a model railway, but sometimes a railway might have to share space with a car. Garages can be cold in winter and it is well worth investing in good quality lighting as well as painting the walls white to provide a clean and comfortable environment. Heating will be necessary in winter too, but the upshot is that a garage provides a sizeable space for a main line model railway ranging from 16ft x 8ft for a single through to 20ft x 20ft for a double. This is *Hornby Magazine's* Topley Dale which now measures 16ft x 10ft with the 'O' gauge test track below.
Mike Wild/*Hornby Magazine*.

If you intend to include gradients, ideally these should not exceed 1-in-30, so that trains maintain traction, and even then restrictions for the load may be necessary. There are products available to help with gradients including DCC Concepts' Powerbase range of metal baseplates and neo magnets. The baseplates sit beneath the track sleepers and the magnets are fixed to the base of the locomotives, which helps improve adhesion.

Storage options

Remember to design in your storage requirements, whether as part of the overall scenic section, or a separate 'off-scene' area. You may wish to incorporate them into your continuous loop scheme at strategic locations with carriage sidings, goods yards and locomotive depots. They could be sandwiched 'off-scene' between two tunnel sections, for example, or as a separate series of dead-end sidings. If you are planning an end-to-end scenario, you may wish to include a storage yard board at one or both ends.

These storage yards also provide your trains with added purpose in our virtual model railway reality, as they offer an origin and destination point to/from the perceived rail network. Each of these storage boards can be as simple as a fan of sidings fed by a series of turnouts, such as a three-way point, for example, or maybe a rotating sector plate that swivels to allow trains to be selected and stored without the need for any points. In addition, this style of storage board can be further developed to rotate so that any locomotive hauled trains can be turned for their return journey, if space allows.

One thing to bear in mind if you opt for this latter design of storage yard - you will need to consider the overhang of the board itself, as it rotates. This could be a good use for an alcove area in a room. Alternatively, you could opt for a sliding traverser style of storage yard, where the board features a series of plain storage lines and can be slid into position via a set of below board runners to select each track.

Whilst a permanent layout isn't necessarily constrained by convention when track laying and wiring, it is worth considering placement of track across baseboard joins, particularly turnouts, so the layout can be dismantled easily should it be necessary in the future. Turnouts should be kept away from baseboard joins and strengthening battens, where possible, to aid installation of point motors below the baseboard. Also, remember to allow for access to your layout. If your scheme is designed to run in a circle along four walls of a room, for example, don't forget to leave space for any doors that open into the room or shed, and perhaps incorporate a lift-out or hinged section which will allow you to enter and exit the hobby room without having to bend down, otherwise it will quickly become a chore and also difficult to manoeuvre objects/furniture/boxes.

So, with all these factors considered, we can progress to drawing up a plan… ■

USEFUL LINKS

- The Federation of Master Builders offers a comprehensive guide to what you need to consider when planning a loft conversion. See www.fmb.org.uk
- For more on planning a garden railway, go to www.keymodelworld.com/article/planning-garden-railway
- www.dccconcepts.com
- www.hornby.com
- www.littleloco.co.uk
- www.minervamodelrailways.co.uk
- www.peco-uk.com

SKILLS GUIDE: LAYOUT CONSTRUCTION

DIY BASE
made simple

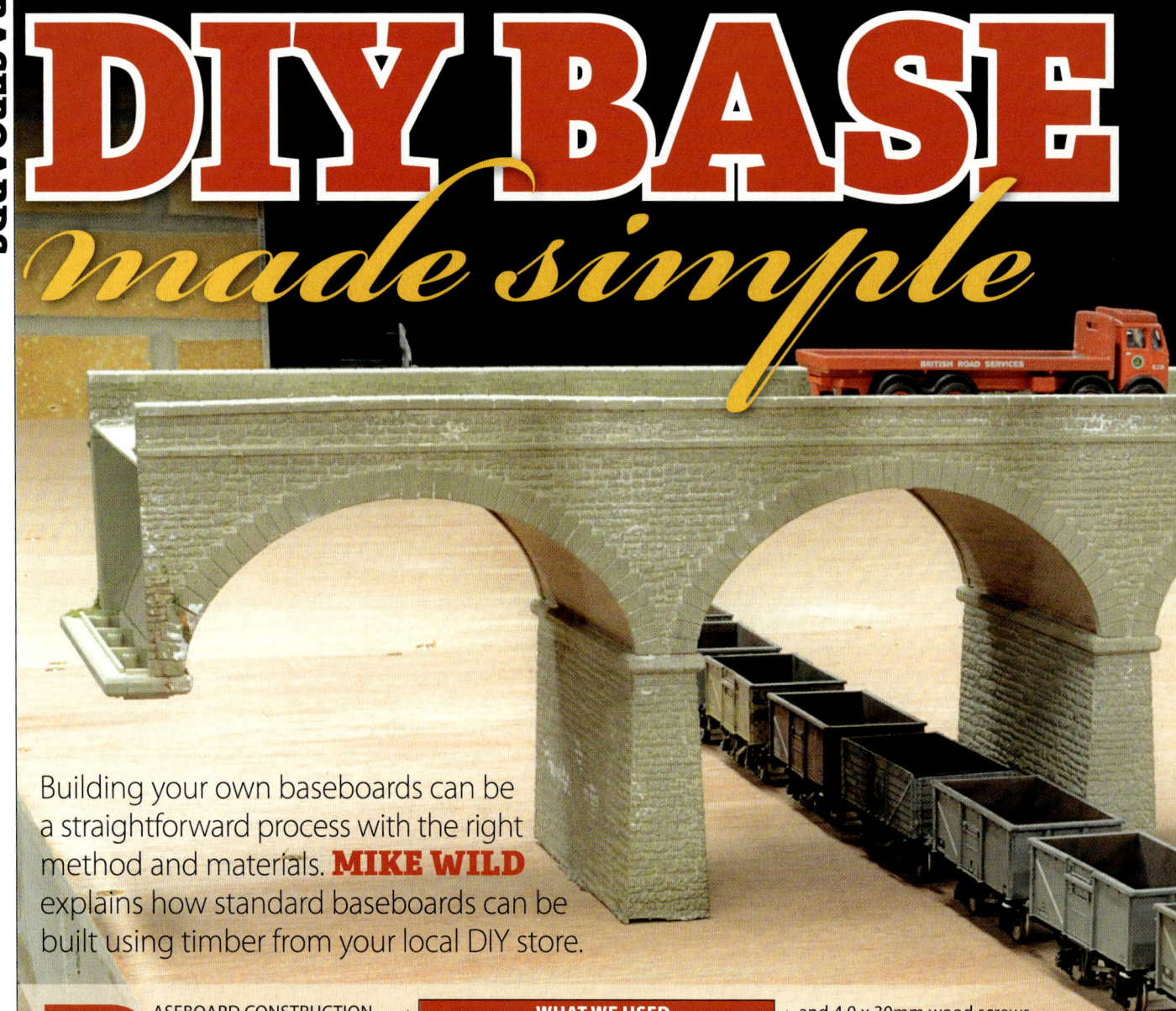

Building your own baseboards can be a straightforward process with the right method and materials. **MIKE WILD** explains how standard baseboards can be built using timber from your local DIY store.

BASEBOARD CONSTRUCTION is a subject which many approach with trepidation, but if you have basic wood working skills – ie, you can use a saw and a screwdriver – making your own boards is well within reach.

Getting this part of a model railway build right is important. A firm, stable and level board will make all the following stages of layout construction straightforward and will contribute greatly to a smooth running railway capable of being used to its best.

When it comes to building baseboards there are several options both in how to build them and what to build them from. For starters there are three primary choices:
• Build your own
• Buy a baseboard kit
• Commission to baseboard builder to build them for you

We start with the DIY board. But what do you build it from? Each potential material has its own positives and negatives but in most cases board tops are made from either plywood or Medium Density Fibreboard (MDF) while framing can either be planed softwood or plywood strips with softwood blocks between.

There are also different styles of baseboard to consider: solid top and open frame. Solid top boards give a level surface across

WHAT WE USED
• 9mm plywood
• 18mm x 69mm planed softwood
• 4.0 x 30mm twin thread wood screws
• No More Nails type adhesive

the length and width and are ideal for building up the scenery above the level of the railway. However, it does preclude adding scenery below the level of the railway - rivers and streams for example.

An open frame design will allow the trackbed to be set above the level of the baseboard frame allowing scenery to rise and fall more naturally. We wouldn't recommend an open frame design for a first DIY baseboard project unless you are proficient with timberwork, so here we are going to focus on a simple solid top design to explain the principals.

We use a standard construction method for our baseboards. These layouts are all portable which means building baseboards in manageable sizes, but the methods we are going to illustrate here can easily be transposed to baseboards of any size with a few modifications. If you plan on creating boards wider than 2ft then extra lengthways supports will be needed to keep the baseboard surface flat and true.

The main ingredients for our boards are 9mm plywood, 18mm x 69mm softwood and 4.0 x 30mm wood screws. All these items are readily available from DIY stores and we highly recommend visiting a store which can cut 8ft x 4ft (2,440mm x 1,220mm) sheets, as this is the most cost-effective way of buying sheet materials.

For this guide, we are a typical 4ft x 2ft solid top baseboard. Only basic tools are required for the job consisting of a saw, electric screwdriver (you can use an ordinary screwdriver but an electric one is a very worthy investment for layout construction), pencil, tape measure and tri-square. You will also need either sandpaper or an electric sander to clean up the cuts.

The golden rule of woodwork is "measure twice, cut once" and using this will keep you out of the worst risk of timber work which is cutting the material short – you can trim over-length timber but not extend under-length cuts!

With baseboard construction it is generally recommended that boards are glued and screwed together, as we are illustrating here. You can use PVA wood glue or a No More Nails adhesive. Both will provide a strong and longstanding joint between the plywood surface and its frame.

So, if you haven't made your own baseboard before, take a look at this guide. You will be surprised how simple it can be. ■

BOARDS

TOOLS
- Hand saw
- Electric screwdriver
- Pencil
- Tape measure
- Tri-square
- 3mm drill bit
- Sandpaper or electric sander

If you can use a saw and a screwdriver, you have the basic skills to build a simple, flat-topped model baseboard such as this. Turn the page to find out how...

SKILLS GUIDE: LAYOUT CONSTRUCTION

STEP BY STEP: DIY BASEBOARDS MADE SIMPLE

1 The raw ingredients for a simple 4ft x 2ft (1,220mm x 610mm) baseboard: a pack of 18mm x 69mm planed softwood in 2,440mm lengths and a cut to size piece of 9mm plywood.

2 The top surface for all of *Hornby Magazine's* exhibition layouts is 9mm plywood – and it has been since our second magazine project. The first was built on 6mm plywood which, while lighter, wasn't as strong.

3 Begin by checking the measurements of the baseboard top – just because the DIY store said it was the size you wanted doesn't mean it will be exact on all four sides. In this case the length was identical on both sides at 1,220mm (4ft).

4 Repeating the process for the width showed that the panel was slightly wider than we had expected. This isn't a problem for this project, but it does mean we need to accommodate this in the cross-members underneath the board.

5 Having confirmed the baseboard top size, we can prepare the timber for the frame. To mark the lengths, use a tri-square and a tape measure for accurate measurements. We set out measurements for the long sides at 1,220mm.

6 Mark the cut position with a pencil using the tri-square then, for future reference, note the length of the cut section on the timber. This helps to ensure the right sections are used for the right area of the board frame.

7 We can now move to cut the long sides using a handsaw. If you are confident with cutting timber you can do it freehand as here or alternatively use a mitre box to ensure a consistent 90 degree angle in each cut.

8 Using the same process the cross-member timbers were cut to size, 576mm, to fit between the outer frame members leading to a 'kit' of components to assemble.

9 Laying the framework out dry means we can check that everything will fit together as planned. This is how the baseboard will look from underneath. Once complete it will be turned over to reveal its smooth and level plywood surface.

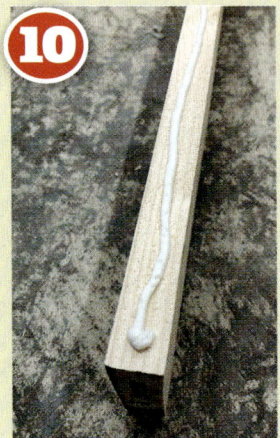

10 To ensure a strong and consistent joint between the baseboard frame and the plywood surface, No More Nails type adhesive was added to the top edge of each frame member. The baseboard surface was then lowered on top of this.

11 Having positioned the first long side timber under the baseboard top, it was then screwed in place with 4.0 x 30mm twin thread wood screws as well as the adhesive.

12 Turning the baseboard over again we can now see the two main frame members in place. The next step is to fit the cross-members which will give the surface full support.

13 With the same adhesive applied to its upper edge and ends, the first cross-member is inserted into position and then screwed in place at the corners through the plywood.

14 We then need to set the positions of the middle two cross members. We standardise on 16in from the outer edge for each of these as we know we can get a drill between the frame should further holes for electrical wiring be needed. Use a tri-square and tape measure for accurate alignment and mark the positions with a pencil.

15 The cross-members can then be put in place using adhesive and screws through the outside face of the main timber using the pencil marks as a guide.

16 To hold the cross-members in place, add a pair of 4.0 x 30mm wood screws on a pencil mark drawn from the original using a tri-square. We will use this pencil mark again when it comes to screwing the top down onto the cross members.

17 To secure the end timbers in place without splitting the wood, drill a pilot hole first with a 3mm drill bit.

18 4.0 x 30mm twin thread wood screws can then be driven in to hold the sides and ends together firmly.

19 Next, using the pencil marks for the cross-members, add a line across the width of the baseboard to denote the position of the cross-member below. Wood screws can then be driven in on this line to screw the baseboard surface to the softwood timber below.

20 Finish off by adding further screws to the end timbers from above and you have finished your first baseboard. While this board measures 1,220mm x 610mm, the same methods can be used for larger or smaller baseboards, but bear in mind that for a wider board an additional brace will be needed in line with the long sides between the cross-members and the outer ends.

21 To join baseboards together we use M6 bolts, 30mm M6 washers and M6 wing nuts. Drill two 7mm diameter holes through the end timbers first to create an opening for the bolts to slot through.

22 Finally insert the bolts with a washer on each side and tighten up with the wing nut ensuring that the baseboard surfaces are aligned above.

SKILLS GUIDE: LAYOUT CONSTRUCTION

LASER CUT BASEBOARDS

TRADITIONAL BASEBOARD assembly calls for a number of tools and, most importantly, an ability to accurately measure and cut timber. Not everyone feels able to build their own baseboards, as cutting straight edges with a hand or power saw isn't always as simple as we would like.

There is a growing number of options to take the hard work out of building baseboards with a number of kits coming to market where all the complex measuring and marking have been done for you. Baseboard kits aren't new, but laser cut designs are becoming increasingly popular. Here, we build one of Tim Horn's laser cut plywood baseboard kits for a 5ft x 1ft board to show you how easy it is.

Tim's range of baseboard kits includes photographic modules, boards with pelmets, a range of sizes and a choice of MDF or plywood finish. Multiple packs are also available and time spent browsing his online catalogue is well worthwhile.

Like flatpack furniture, all the parts arrive neatly packaged in a sturdy cardboard box. Inspection reveals that everything is cut straight and true – better than we ever could with a handsaw – while the actual parts are cut from 6mm plywood offering a strong and light baseboard which would be difficult to make to the standard and rigidity from scratch.

Instructions are available online at www.timhorn.co.uk but most of the process is quite intuitive. You get two sides, four centre cross-braces, two outer and two inner ends, diagonal cross-braces, a top, side covers and packs of screws, bolts and dowels to complete the boards.

We can't emphasise enough here the accuracy of the cut on the parts – everything is precise showing the primary advantage of laser cutting. The parts are all annotated for their inner faces as the cuts are angled for a tight fit so it is important to get the parts the right way round.

So what do you need to assemble one of these boards? Nothing more than PVA wood glue, a screwdriver and a hammer. That's it. Everything else is done for you, so we will let the step by step guide do the talking… ■

Laser cut
BASEBO

TOOLS
» PVA wood glue
» Screwdriver
» Hammer

THE ALTERNATIVES

If the thought of building a baseboard still brings you out in cold sweats, don't worry, there are more options available. A number of manufacturers exist that will build baseboards for you including standard designs as well as bespoke products. Take a look at the following websites for inspiration and advice:

Baseboard.co	www.modelbaseboards.co.uk
DCC Train Automation	www.dcctrainautomation.co.uk
Model Layout Services	www.modellayoutservices.co.uk
Model Rail Baseboards	www.modelrailbaseboards.com
Model Railway Solutions	www.modelrailwaysolutions.co.uk
Modula Layouts	www.modulalayouts.co.uk
Scale Model Scenery	www.scalemodelscenery.co.uk
White Rose Model Works	www.whiterosemodelworks.co.uk

WHAT WE USED

PRODUCT	SUPPLIER	PRICE
5ft x 1ft birch plywood laser cut baseboard kit	tim@timhorn.co.uk	POA

Laser cut baseboards take the hassle out of building your own boards. Assembling this Tim Horn kit took under 30 minutes from start to finish with a little extra time needed for the glue to cure thoroughly following construction. It is now ready to become the basis for a new project layout.

The use of laser cut timber takes a lot of the stress out of baseboard constuction. **MIKE WILD** builds a Tim Horn laser cut baseboard kit and discovers just how easy it is.

SKILLS GUIDE: LAYOUT CONSTRUCTION

STEP BY STEP: ASSEMBLING A LASER CUT BASEBOARD

1 On opening the box you are greeted with a complete kit ready for assembly. There is no cutting, sanding, adjustment or measuring – you just put the parts together.

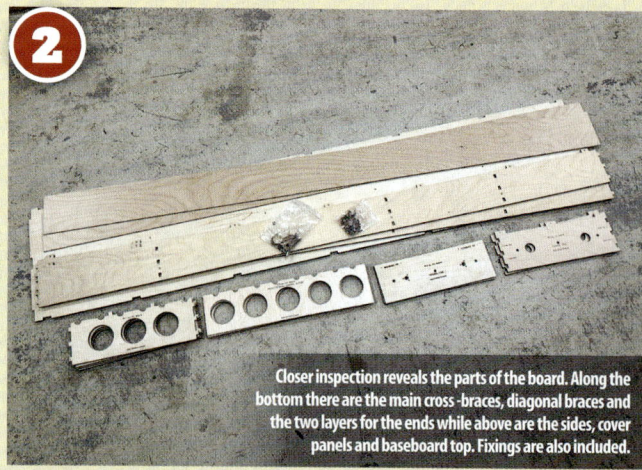

2 Closer inspection reveals the parts of the board. Along the bottom there are the main cross-braces, diagonal braces and the two layers for the ends while above are the sides, cover panels and baseboard top. Fixings are also included.

3 This kit is made from 6mm plywood, but it is also available in Medium Density Fibreboard for a lower price. All of the cross-braces are pre-cut to accommodate wiring at the top through the half-round cuts as well as having large open circles cut in the cross-braces for wiring to pass through.

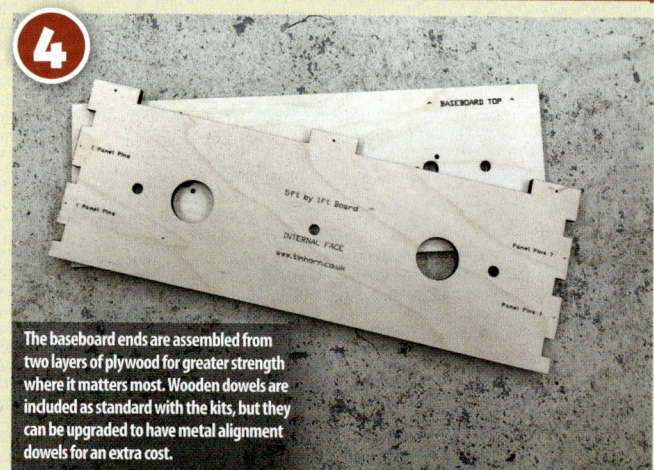

4 The baseboard ends are assembled from two layers of plywood for greater strength where it matters most. Wooden dowels are included as standard with the kits, but they can be upgraded to have metal alignment dowels for an extra cost.

5 The kit parts are designed to slot together, but it is important to ensure that the parts are fitted with the internal faces (marked on each piece) facing the right way for the best fit. All screw holes are countersunk and where nails are required alignment holes are pre-drilled too.

6 Assembly starts with the cross-braces. Run a bead of PVA glue along the top edge and position the tabs into the slots on the underside of the baseboard surface. Repeat for the other cross-braces, working from the centre outwards then join one of the side panels to them.

7 To ensure consistent joints, a single screw goes through the baseboard side panel into the cross-brace. This is pre-drilled and countersunk, as can be seen by the joining point to the baseboard top.

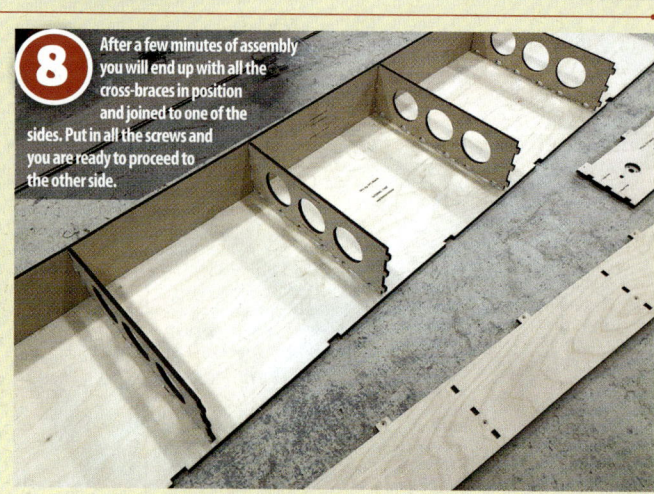

8 After a few minutes of assembly you will end up with all the cross-braces in position and joined to one of the sides. Put in all the screws and you are ready to proceed to the other side.

9 Adding the second side couldn't be simpler – turn the board over, apply PVA wood glue to its edges and the edges of the cross-braces, position and fit the supplied screws.

10 Screws are also provided for the centreline of the baseboard surface to screw down into the cross-braces.

11 Now the ends can be fitted using the same routine – glue, screw and then hammer the supplied panel pins in through the marks at each side.

12 Adding the inner layer of the ends is simple. Apply PVA glue to the joining surface, position behind the outer layer then insert the supplied M6 bolts to help the glue bond fully. Repeat at the other end.

13 Wooden alignment dowels are provided as standard with the kits, but metal versions can be substituted. We opted to leave these off the board for the time being, as we have a plan for its future.

14 With the main components assembled, we added the diagonal braces underneath next to ensure the board remains strong and stable. These are simply glued in place with PVA wood glue.

15 To complete the board, we added the plywood fascia panels which neatly hide the screws and fixings through the sides. PVA glue was spread across the length of the joining surface…

16 …and to ensure a consistent join between the two surfaces, the fascia was weighted down with glue and paint tins and left to cure. All that is left to do now is apply the other fascia and give the board a coat of paint to seal the wood as recommended by the manufacturer. Then it's ready for railway construction.

SKILLS GUIDE: LAYOUT CONSTRUCTION

DIGITAL COMMAND CONTROL

Forming the plan... making it reality

You've decided what you want to model and you know where you're going to build it. But how do you turn your vision into reality? **MIKE WILD** explains all.

I'VE ALWAYS LOVED railway yards. I used to pass Healey Mills yard, near Wakefield, on my way to school but I could only glimpse it from a distance. I also remember being captivated by Bescot yard, visible from the M6 motorway, not to mention countless other yards fleetingly glimpsed from the train window.

The Great Central Railway between Loughborough and Leicester North has something else that's always appealed to me, too. Most preserved railways use rural branch line – or secondary main lines – as their basis. Not the GCR – this was once a premier main line, linking London to Nottingham, via Rugby and Leicester.

What was originally called the Great Central Railway's 'London Extension', it was the last great main line railway to be built in Britain until the Channel Tunnel Rail Link in the 2000s. The 'London Extension', therefore, holds a special place in British railway history.

Many mourn its closure in 1966. It was the infamous Dr Beeching who instigated its closure.

What made the 'London Extension' a particular magnet for enthusiasts was the richness of its train services. You had named expresses (the 'Master Cutler'), local 'stoppers' and lots of goods trains, moving coal, fish and steel.

The GCR became part of the LNER at the Grouping in 1923. It fell under the Eastern Region of British Railways at Nationalisation in 1948. From 1958, however, the 'London Extension' passed into the hands of BR's London Midland Region. Therefore, the line hosted a mix of LNER and LMS motive power – not to mention British Railways' own designs of steam and diesel locomotives and multiple units.

Ex-Great Western Railway locomotives and stock were common visitors too and it was not uncommon to occasionally see Southern Region locomotives and coaches either. Factor in that London Transport shared the route between Quainton Road in Buckinghamshire to a point close to Marylebone station in London and you can see why it was such a favourite for enthusiasts.

You won't find Quorn Magna in any book about the GCR 'London Extension' but by studying trackplans of real stations, you can take enough key features to create something fictional though thoroughly convincing.

A group of enthusiasts got together in the late 1960s to try to save as much of the 'London Extension' as possible. The result is an 8 1/4mile south from Loughborough to just beyond the former station at Belgrave & Birstall. Here, a new station called Leicester North has been created.

Fittingly called the Great Central Railway, it's an almost perfect re-creation of British main line of yesteryear. Goods trains, mail trains – not to mention passenger trains – are a common sight on the restored double track. The GCR also has an enviable collection of locomotives, coaches and wagons, some of which once worked on the line in the old days.

This operational variety will always make for a superb layout. You'll never get bored operating it.

When we at Hornby Magazine needed a new project, we had a 16ft by 8ft space to play with. We've long wanted to capture the operational potential of the GCR.

On the preserved railway between Quorn and Rothley is Swithland Sidings. It's an expansive goods yard that, since 2012, has been fully signalled with ex-GWR/Western Region lower quadrant semaphores. The sidings host all manner of rolling stock, from 16ton mineral wagons to Travelling Post Office vans and even carriages awaiting restoration. Exactly what I find exciting about railway yards!

WHAT WE USED		
PRODUCT	MANUFACTURER	CAT NO.
GCR gentlemen's toilet	Scenecraft	44-115A
GCR waiting room	Scenecraft	44-116A
GCR booking office and canopy	Scenecraft	44-117A
GCR high level station entrance	Scenecraft	44-119A
GCR single track road bridge	Scenecraft	44-121
GCR island platform sections	Scenecraft	44-153
GCR island platform ramps	Scenecraft	44-0008
Weybourne road bridge	Scenecraft	44-0072
Peco code 75 bullhead track	Peco	SL-108F
Peco code 75 bullhead left-hand point	Peco	SLU-1188
Peco code 75 bullhead right-hand point	Peco	SLU-1189
Peco code 75 bullhead rail joiners	Peco	SL-114
Peco code 75 bullhead buffer stops	Peco	SL-1140

Swithland's appeal settled the matter. We would fill our 16ft by 8ft space with a Great Central Railway-inspired 'OO' gauge layout.

Now, 16ft by 8ft might seem like a big space, especially if you've only got a little box room to play with. But it's actually quite a small space in which to re-create a main line such as the 'London Extension'.

Unless you're blessed with a spare room the size of an aircraft hangar, getting any prototype location to fit will require you to carefully pick and choose key elements.

The design started with the concept of a station on one side and a hidden storage yard on the other. This is a classic, exhibition-style arrangement. However, we soon felt that the plan would be too restrictive. If we went for a full, four-sided design, we could replicate Swithland Sidings on the other.

Many of our design cues are taken from the preserved section of the GCR. However, while it takes inspiration from what remains today, we didn't have the space to replicate every inch of track. After many hours of research using the prototype track plans available at the Railway Archive (www.railwaysarchive.co.uk), we have a track plan that gives a realistic flavour of the GCR that fits our space without it being a slavish copy.

SKILLS GUIDE: LAYOUT CONSTRUCTION

While we've listed the possible locomotives you could use on a Great Central Railway-based layout, don't forget that you need to think about rolling stock too. You'll need Eastern, London Midland, Western and Southern Region coaches plus plenty of wagons – and there are plenty of wagons for you to choose from!

Our station is called Quorn Magna – a combination of Quorn & Woodhouse and Ashby Magna. It takes much of its inspiration from the preserved station at Quorn and it's a good starting point because Bachmann has included its station buildings as part of its Scenecraft range of ready-made buildings.

Highlights include an island platform, a siding stretching back from the platform on the outer circuit, a good yard with two long sidings and inclusion of a goods loop and headshunt. At the country end of the station side, the line curves around - one of our compromises of making a model railway - with the double track main line running between the lie-by siding and headshunt until it reaches a road overbridge.

This is another Bachmann Scenecraft product. It's not based on a GCR prototype – it's actually based on a bridge at Weybourne on the North Norfolk Railway – but it's closely related to bridge styles on the GCR and will save many hours of scratchbuilding a true replica.

After the bridge, the line continues its curve around to the other side by crossing a lower level board which will ultimately model Swithland Reservoir, though with the railway on a curve rather than straight. It curves towards our take on Swithland Sidings.

Again, to build Swithland Sidings in full would require a much larger space than the 16ft by 2ft area that we have available in this project. Naturally there are compromises and adjustments to the track plan, but we hope that what you see will feel as representative of the location as we think it is.

The main fixtures are the double track main line splitting into four to provide Up and Down goods loops either side. The outer circuit Down goods loop is the only additional track on that circuit, but we have also introduced an incorrect, but equally useful in modelling terms, facing crossover to one end of the scene to allow trains to run from the outside circuit directly into the Up line loop or in fact the yard itself.

The goods yard has four long sidings heading back towards the reservoir end while an additional two short lines, which aren't at the real location, are included for storage of a DMU or spare locomotives. Like the facing crossover, these are aimed at increasing the operational flexibility for the layout as a model railway.

QUORN MAGNA LOCOMOTIVE FLEET	
Eastern Region, 1950-1958	
Locomotive	Manufacturer
Robinson 'O4' 2-8-0	Bachmann
Robinson 'D11' 4-4-0	Bachmann
Gresley 'K3' 2-6-0	Bachmann
Gresley 'V2' 2-6-2	Bachmann
Gresley 'A3' 4-6-2	Hornby
Thompson 'O1' 2-8-0	Hornby
Thompson 'B1' 4-6-0	Hornby
Robinson 'J11' 0-6-0	Bachmann
Thompson 'O1' 2-8-0	Hornby
Thompson 'L1' 2-6-4T	Hornby
Midland Region, 1958-1966	
Locomotive	Manufacturer
Stanier '8F' 2-8-0	Hornby
Stanier 'Black Five' 4-6-0	Hornby
Rebuilt 'Royal Scot' 4-6-0	Hornby
Riddles 'Britannia' 4-6-2	Hornby
Riddles '5MT' 4-6-0	Bachmann
Riddles 'WD' 2-8-0	Bachmann
Riddles '9F' 2-10-0	Bachmann/Hornby
Collett 'Hall' 4-6-0	Bachmann/Hornby
Bulleid 'West Country' 4-6-2	Hornby
Preservation, 2024	
Robinson 'O4' 2-8-0 63601	Bachmann
Bulleid 'West Country' 4-6-2 34039	Hornby
Stanier 'Black Five' 45305/45491	Hornby
Maunsell 'King Arthur' 4-6-0 30777	Hornby
Riddles 'Britannia' 4-6-2 70013	Hornby
Hawksworth '6959' 4-6-0 6990	Bachmann
Riddles '5MT' 4-6-0 73156	Bachmann
Riddles '2MT' 2-6-0 78018/019	Hornby
Ivatt '2MT' 2-6-0 46521	Bachmann
Fowler 'Jinty' 0-6-0T 47406	Bachmann
Stanier '8F' 2-8-0 48624/48305	Hornby
Riddles '9F' 2-10-0 92214	Bachmann/Hornby
Hunslet 'Austerity' 0-6-0ST 68067	EFE
Class 08 0-6-0DE 13101/D4137	Bachmann/Hornby
Class 20 Bo-Bo D8098	Bachmann
Class 25/1 Bo-Bo D5185	Bachmann/Heljan
Class 27 Bo-Bo D5401	Heljan
Class 31 A1A-A1A D5830	Accurascale/Bachmann/Hornby
Class 33 Bo-Bo D6535	Heljan
Class 37 Co-Co D6700/37714	Accurascale/Bachmann
Class 45 1Co-Co1 D123	Heljan
Class 47 Co-Co D1705	Bachmann/Heljan
Class 50 Co-Co 50017	Accurascale/Hornby
Class 101 DMU 50203/50266/ 50321/51427	Bachmann
Class 122 railcar 55009	Dapol

There are two further compromises at the reservoir end of the track plan. First is that the road underbridge hasn't been included due to space limitations while the tracks also don't split quite as far apart as they do at the real location in this area to suit the track plan. On the Up side, the Mountsorrel branch connection has been included and in time we envisage that this will be extended off the scenic boards to a small off-scene storage siding behind the reservoir board.

Try new things

Designing a layout doesn't just mean devising a trackplan. It also gives you the opportunity to try new things. For example, this was the first layout we have built using Peco's Code 75 bullhead track.

As we explain elsewhere in this publication, traditional 'OO' gauge track is a little compromised. Sleepers are too small and too closely spaced and while much of the railway now used flatbottom rail, the majority of steam-era lines were laid with bullhead rail. The curves of traditional section track are also tighter than prototypical.

Peco's bullhead points are to a more prototypical radius and we have used them throughout, except for three curved points, which create the facing crossover at the station end of the yard. These were another necessary compromise to get the trackplan to fit the space.

However, the remaining points are all left- and right-hand large radius bullhead rail turnouts which use what Peco calls its Unifrog design. This means that the point 'frog' – the vee at the centre of the crossing – is completely isolated from the rest of the point with its own wire attached. The point can be installed and used as supplied but if you have short wheelbase locomotives, we recommend that you add the frog switching ability to these points for reliable running. We added this using the frog switching output built into the DCC Concepts Cobalt IP digital point motors that we have used under the layout.

Plain track is entirely Peco's bullhead flexible track. We found it easy to work with and more flexible than traditional flat bottom rail. The only time this was an issue was when we first reassembled the layout. As the main lines had only been loosely pinned, heat had distorted

SKILLS GUIDE: LAYOUT CONSTRUCTION

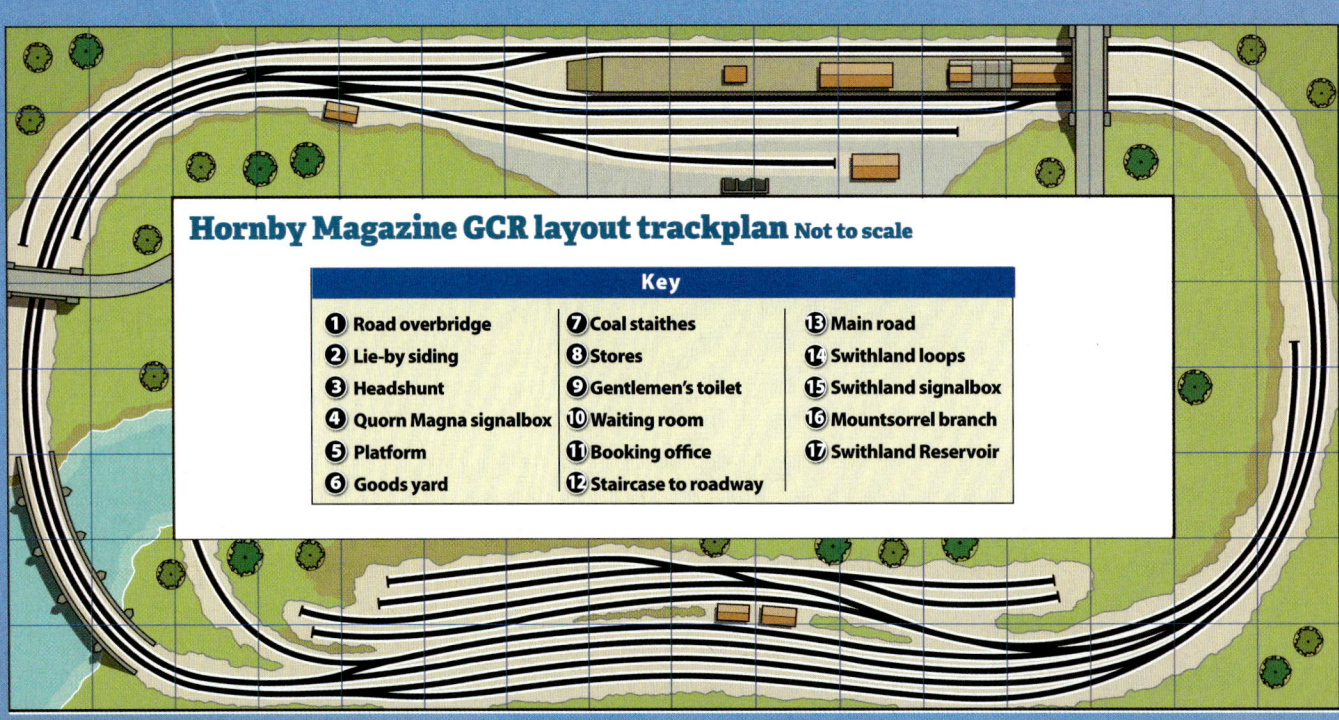

Hornby Magazine GCR layout trackplan Not to scale

Key

❶ Road overbridge	❼ Coal staithes	⓭ Main road
❷ Lie-by siding	❽ Stores	⓮ Swithland loops
❸ Headshunt	❾ Gentlemen's toilet	⓯ Swithland signalbox
❹ Quorn Magna signalbox	❿ Waiting room	⓰ Mountsorrel branch
❺ Platform	⓫ Booking office	⓱ Swithland Reservoir
❻ Goods yard	⓬ Staircase to roadway	

the rails which meant a little adjustment and trimming of the track to fit as it should.

Another strong point of the bullhead track system is the rail joiner design. These tiny items actually look like real four-bolt fishplates. However, a word of caution as we have found that their electrical conductivity isn't always the best, so it is worth feeding the track section separately for absolute reliability. In some cases, we were able to work around this by running solder into the rail joiner to make a permanent electrical bond.

Operation

It's imperative that you try to build in how the layout will operate at the design stage. There's nothing worse than building a layout and then finding that you can't carry out all the manoeuvres you want to. At best, you'll find yourself constantly frustrated with it; at worst, you'll rip up all your hard work and start again.

Our track plan offers several possibilities for train storage and running. At Quorn Magna, goods trains can be reversed into the outer circuit siding to allow passenger trains to pass while the inner circuit goods loop provides access to the main line and the goods yard headshunt.

xxxxxxxxxxxx

The layout was build using laser-cut baseboard kits (see pxx for more). We modified one of boards by adding 12mm MDF panels to two sides, enabling it to be lowered. We will build the reservoir scene here.

While the reservoir scenic section is not yet complete, we had to create a trackbed across the lowered area in order to run trains. A new railway deck was cut to shape from 6mm MDF and mounted on temporary blocks of 12mm MDF. This will be clad to look like a viaduct.

This is why the GCR appeals to modellers: it gives you an excuse to run whatever you like! This is the post-1958 era when the 'London Extension' came under London Midland Region control, enabling you to run '9Fs' and 'Royal Scots'.

Another convincing 'London Extension' scene, as 'Black Fives' were regulars in later years. A pristine 44694 waits to depart with a rake of matching BR lined maroon Mk 1s.

USEFUL LINKS	
Accurascale	www.accurascale.com
Bachmann/EFE	www.bachmann.co.uk
Dapol	www.dapol.co.uk
Heljan	www.heljan.co.uk
Hornby	www.hornby.com
Peco	www.peco-uk.com
Gaugemaster	www.gaugemasterretail.com
SLW	railexclusive.com/suttons-loco-works/

DIGITAL COMMAND CONTROL

SKILLS GUIDE: LAYOUT CONSTRUCTION

DIGITAL COMMAND CONTROL

This is why a layout such as this demands Digital Command Control. Two trains pass each other on the main line while a third shunts the yard at Swithland.

The track arrangement allows a goods train to arrive in the goods loop, be shunted into the sidings, reformed and then continue its journey. Alternatively, after shunting, the locomotive could run around the train, propel it out of the station loop and then use the crossover to return down the line to Swithland Sidings.

Passenger trains are limited to five coaches to match the loop length at the station and at Swithland which allows them to be held to allow for operation of other trains on the main line circuits. Equally, goods trains are kept to a maximum of 20 four-wheel goods wagons (excluding brake van) to fit within the loops and sidings.

At Swithland we have included a facing crossover so trains from the outer circuit can cross directly into the sidings at Swithland which, while not prototypically correct, does introduce additional flexibility to the track plan.

Digital Command Control is a must for a layout such as this. To control this layout using traditional 12V DC analogue control (see pxx) would require so many isolating section that the underside of the layout would be a veritable jungle of wires.

You can read more about DCC on pxx but, effectively, it means that the whole layout is permanently live and the trains can move anywhere at any time when the decoders inside them receive specific digital signals sent out from the control system. It's the closest way that a model railway can be operated to mimic the real thing as technology allows.

We used Gaugemaster Prodigy control system and our wiring method is simple but robust. Red and black dropper wires connected to each section of track (red to the outside rail, black to the inside) which are then joined to what's called a 'main power bus' which runs around the layout to distribute power to all of the features. Point motors and signals are all powered from the same bus wire for simplicity.

Motive power

We debated whether we should model the BR era or the preservation period. Luckily, the major manufacturers offer enough products to easily do both.

During its lifetime, the line played host to a huge variety of locomotives and rolling stock. Of the Great Central Railway's own designs, only the 'Director' 4-4-0, '9J' 0-6-0 and '8K' 2-8-0s (all Bachmann) and the '9N' 4-6-2Ts (Sonic/Rails of Sheffield) are available ready-to-run.

The LNER era is represented by Gresley's 'A1/A3' 4-6-2s (Hornby), Gresley 'V2' 2-6-2s (Bachmann), Thompson 'B1' 4-6-0s (Hornby/Bachmann), Thompson 'O1' 2-8-0s (Hornby), Thompson 'L1' 2-6-4Ts (Hornby). The bulk of models for the LMR period comes from Hornby ('Black Five' 4-6-0s, rebuilt 'Royal Scot' 4-6-0s, '8F' 2-8-0s, 'Britannia' 4-6-2s and '9F' 2-10-0s) while Bachmann offers the BR '5MT' 4-6-0 and the '9F', as well as suitable DMU classes.

The core of the preservation era can be modelled using ready-to-run products (see panel). One of the joys of modelling the preservation era is that a railway such as the

GCR regularly hires in guest engines and so this layout could play host to anything from GNR 'Stirling Single' No. 1 to new-build 'A1' 4-6-2 Tornado. Another plus for re-creating the preservation era is that the GCR has been used to test new trains for the national network including the Class 73/9 rebuilds, bi-mode Class 769 units (rebuilt Class 319s) and GBRf Class 66s.

As you can see, the GCR in preservation is an exciting place to replicate in model form. We've only touched on the subjects you could model and it is well worth adding your own research if you want to model the line to expand upon the list we have here.

Building this layout has been an entertaining and rewarding exercise.

The biggest debate now is whether the layout should remain in the BR era or whether we should roll the clock forward to the present day in preservation? The jury is out on that decision, but maybe we should invest in a second set of buildings so we can ring the changes when we want to? ∎

Top Tip!

We used layers of expanding foam to create the landscape around the railway. Invert the can during spraying for the best performance and working layers. The foam can be shaped using a saw or hot wire foam before being covered with masking tape, followed by layers of paper coated with PVA. This makes for a quick and cheap landscaping method.

The Swithland Siding area is designed to capture the feel of the real location without being a 100% prototypical copy. The track was laid and 'tested' before any scenic work started, just to make sure the plan worked.

We used Peco bullhead track – almost – throughout. The rail joiners look like real fishplates but electrical continuity needs beefing up. The points are Unifrogs – but we recommend that you add the frog switching ability to these points for reliable running.

As this layout will attend exhibitions, the final sleeper before each side of each baseboard joint was cut away and DCC Concepts pre-etched sleepers to be pinned to the baseboard and soldered to the rails. This help maintain rail alignment each time the layout is dismantled and reassembled.

SUBSCRIBE TODAY!

SAVE OVER £22.00

From the Publisher
Mike Wild

Here at *Hornby Magazine* we are all at the heart of the hobby and in every issue we bring you the latest model railway news, product reviews and features you won't find anywhere else.

Each issue of the magazine is packed full of inspirational modelling articles from our dedicated team to give you all the information you need to build your own model railway or inform you about your next purchase.

Don't miss out on this great subscription offer.

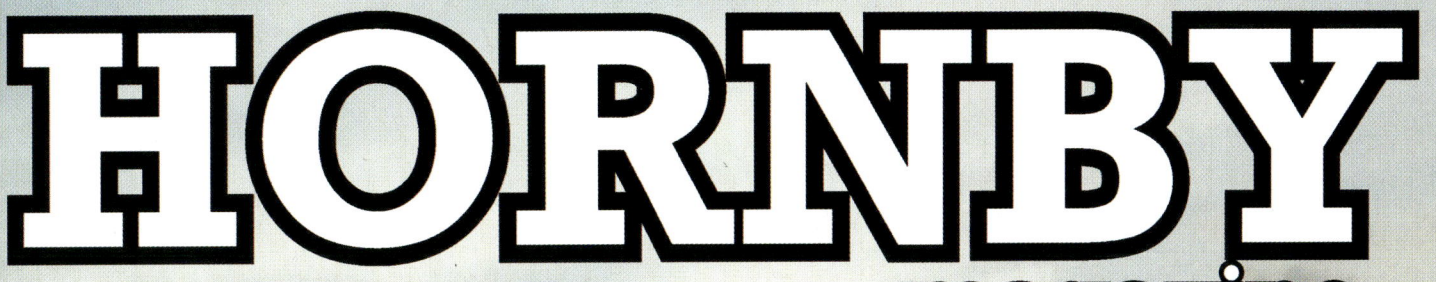

WRITTEN BY MODELLERS FOR MODELLERS OF ALL SKILL LEVELS, *HORNBY MAGAZINE* TAKES A UNIQUE APPROACH TO MODEL RAILWAYS

PRINT ONLY SUBSCRIPTION

ONLY £46.99
by annual Direct Debit

Please quote: **HM2024** when ordering

SUBSCRIBER BENEFITS
✓ **DELIVERED DIRECT** to your door
✓ **SAVE** over buying individual issues
✓ **EXCLUSIVE DISCOUNTS** on the *Key Publishing* Shop
✓ **SUBSCRIBER DISCOUNTS** on *Key Publishing* event tickets
✓ **BE THE FIRST** to read the latest features

VISIT THE **KEY MODEL WORLD SHOP** FOR THE LATEST OFFERS

Total cost of 12 issues of *Hornby Magazine* Exact subscription savings totalling £22.01

SCAN THE QR CODE TO ORDER DIRECT FROM OUR SHOP
shop.keymodelworld.com/hmsubs

or call **+44 (0)1780 480404** (Lines open 9.00-5.30, Monday-Friday GMT)

Terms and conditions: Quoted rates are for UK subscriptions only, paying by Annual Direct Debit. Quoted savings based on those rates versus purchasing individual print and digital issues. Standard one-year print subscription prices: UK - £55.99, EU - £71.99, USA - £74.99, ROW - £77.99.
CLOSING DATE: 31st December 2024 *(prices may change in the upcoming year)*

SKILLS GUIDE: LAYOUT CONSTRUCTION

Model railway ELECTRICS

Getting the basics of model railway electrics right is essential for a smooth running railway. **MIKE WILD** presents top tips to make your layout work faultlessly every time you turn the power on.

MODEL RAILWAY ELECTRICS are an essential part of a working layout and with a few simple techniques everyone can install wiring to bring their railway to life and keep the wires concealed out of view.

The term 'electrics' scares many modellers, but the simple truth is that all circuits on a model railway are a repetition of the same basic positive and negative feed. So long as you maintain an air of calm and sense when installing your wiring and keep track of what you have done, the process of wiring a railway should be very straightforward.

There are two main types of control system available today – DC (analogue) which uses a 12v DC controller to supply power to the track when the control knob is turned and DCC (digital) which provides a constant 15v AC current to the track and sends electrical signals to a decoder (a small computer chip) installed inside a locomotive. Both have their merits and cost implications, and you can read our Digital Basics guide on pages 44-49.

What we aim to do here is arm you with the basics and understanding so that you can begin wiring your own layout for either control system with the right methods. ■

Wiring can be a daunting prospect, but it doesn't have to be. Take your time, plan your wire routes accordingly and above all keep it neat with colour coding. These are some of the essentials for wiring a model railway: 7/0.2 equipment wire for track connections, 28/0.2 bell wire for power for power bus feeds, soldering iron, plug-in terminal blocks and wire strippers.

KEEP IT SIMPLE

When it comes to wiring it is easy to get in a mess. However, with a little planning and a 'keep it simple' attitude wiring up a model railway is within the abilities of everyone.

For *Hornby Magazine*'s layouts, we have a standard scheme of wire colouring to make it easy to follow what we are doing. For an analogue layout the outer main line on a double track circuit is always wired with red and black wire (red to the outer rail and black to the inner) while the inner circuit is wired with yellow and blue wire (yellow to the outer rail and blue to the inner). Further to this we use green and orange for point motor power feeds and white for the common return feed.

For accessories such as lighting, we standardise on brown and white wiring (with the two wires spun together) meaning that we always know which circuit a pair of wires is intended for.

There is also a lot to be said for keeping wiring neat and tidy. A box of cable clips is

a great addition to your toolbox as it means that wiring can be run around the inside of the baseboard framing neatly and without the chance of it snagging after installation.

CHOOSING THE RIGHT WIRE

Sourcing the right type of wire for the job in hand is essential. There are two main groups for electrical wire – single core and multi-core. Single core consists of a single strand of copper wire and while this does have some applications, it is susceptible to failure through bending resulting in electrical failures.

By far the best option is multi-core wire which features several strands of copper wire together inside the plastic insulation. This type of wire is much more flexible and long lasting and can be used for almost any purpose on a model railway. For our track feeds we use 7/0.2mm multi-core wire (seven strands each with a diameter of 0.2mm) which we have always found to be reliable through years of exhibition layout operation.

Wire is available on reels from suppliers such as Rapid Electronics, Squires Tools and others. It is often cheaper to buy in bulk than in short lengths and it is better to have more wire available for future development than be splicing in varied colours to finish a cable.

DIGITAL POWER BUS

Digital layout wiring is a little different to an analogue layout. In the case of the latter each circuit is independent meaning that it needs its own wiring, but when it comes to digital layouts all circuits can operate from the same main circuit – the power bus.

The power bus carries all the signals from the digital controller around the layout and needs to be more substantial than the 7/0.2 strand multi-core wire we used for track connections. In our case, we use a 28 strand multi-core cable which is connected to strategic connector blocks to distribute power to individual track sections. The beauty of digital is that no switches are required so you can keep on repeating the same circuit from the power bus to deliver power to the entire track formation.

CHOOSING A SOLDERING IRON

A soldering iron is essential for model railway wiring and especially if you wish to install neat and almost invisible wiring on your layout. The best type to go for when starting out is a 25watt soldering iron which will provide plenty of heat to melt solder and fix wires to rails and other components without any fuss. Buy a stand with the iron and a cleaning sponge, as it is essential to keep the iron nib in first rate condition for the best possible joints.

ESSENTIAL TOOLS

Only a handful of tools are needed for model railway wiring. Our tool box consists of a 25watt soldering iron, a pair of adjustable wire strippers to suit different wire gauges, a pair of side cutters (for cutting wire to length) and a screwdriver. Beyond this all you really need is wire, switches and plug-in terminal blocks!

INSULATED AND LIVE FROG POINTS

When it comes to points and electrics there are two different types commonly available – insulated frog and live frog points. Insulated frog points have an insulated section at the 'V' of the point frog which simplifies them electrically as they require no additional wiring to create a loop. However, because of that insulated section – albeit only a few millimetres long – short wheelbase locomotives are more prone to stalling as there is an unpowered section in the centre of the point.

Live frog points – often referred to under Peco's brand name Electrofrog =– are metal throughout and remove the chance of

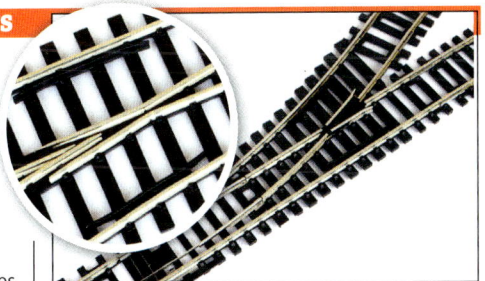

locomotives stalling. However, they require a little more planning when it comes to electrical feeds as a loop will require insulated rail joiners in one position along its length to avoid a short circuit.

SKILLS GUIDE: LAYOUT CONSTRUCTION

KNOW YOUR POINT FEEDS

When installing a point, it is essential that it is always fed electrically from the toe end. If not it will cause an electrical short. For facing points, it is important to separate them electrically at the point that they join to avoid electrical shorts. These basic rules need to be applied to all points to ensure that a model railway works correctly when power is applied.

A Points must be fed electrically from the toe end, as indicated on this Peco code 75 medium radius right hand turnout.

B When creating a crossover the join between the two points must be made with insulated rail joiners to prevent short circuits.

C In this simple fan of sidings, all of the points are fed electrically from the bottom of the image. As the point blades are set for the route, the power is sent to the correct line.

D In the same set of loops, all the lines have double insulated rail joiners part way along as required for the use of live frog points. This is to prevent power from being supplied from both ends of the loop and causing a short circuit at the point frogs.

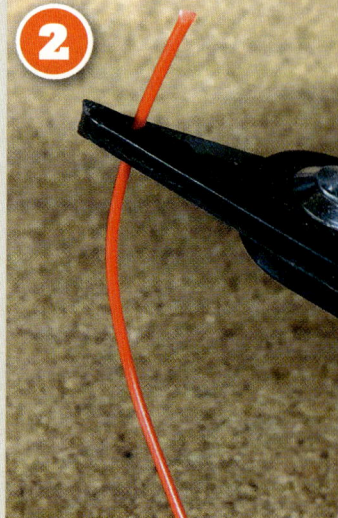

Drill a 2mm diameter hole for each wire you wish to connect to the track between a pair of sleeper ends.

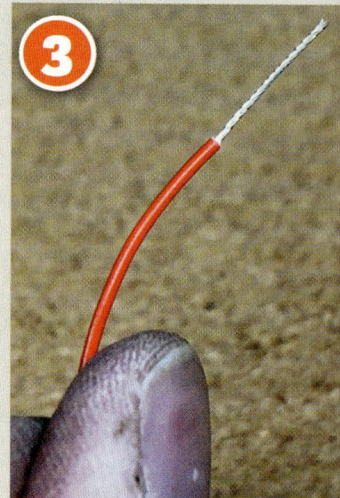

Using a pair of wire strippers, bare the end of the insulation from the wire removing around 15mm-20mm of the plastic covering.

When using multi-core wire twist the newly stripped strands together to create a single cable, otherwise it will be difficult to solder the wire to the rail.

MODEL RAILWAY ELECTRICS RULES

No mains electricity
Buy a professionally-made power supply for your model railway and only use low-voltage (12v to 16v) outputs. Do not be tempted to run a mains cable along your layout. Mains voltage can, and does, kill.

Keep notes
This is all about making it easy for yourself in future. Make sketches of the wiring noting where the wires go and what they do. Ideally you should number each end of each wire with a label so that if they are ever disconnected, either by design or accident, you can establish where they should go.

Use the right tools
Using the correct tool ensures that the task is done effectively and efficiently. As an example, use a wire stripper to strip the insulating sleeve off lengths of wire.

Keep it tidy
Keeping your wiring tidy will help you when it comes to locating faults or making changes.

Colour code your wiring
A simple colour code can make it much easier to work out what wire goes where. If your track feeds are all red for one side and black for the other it makes it much harder to introduce a short circuit.

SOLDERING WIRES ONTO RAILS

Using multi-core wire it is a simple process to solder a wire to a rail to provide an electrical connection. You will need a 25watt soldering iron and stand, electrical solder, an electric drill with a 2mm or 2.5mm drill bit, wire strippers and multi-core wire...

4 Warm up the soldering iron and apply a small amount of solder to the tip of the soldering iron and heating the wire at the same time. Avoid excessive heat on the wire as it will melt the insulation. This process is called tinning.

5 Tin the side of the rail by using the soldering iron to melt a small amount of solder on the rail side. This completes preparation for the final joint.

6 Above: Hold the wire against the rail in the position you wish to solder it. Apply the soldering iron to the tinned wire and previously tinned rail. Allow the solder to melt and fuse with the rail. Leave to set (a matter of seconds at room temperature) and your connection is done.

7 Left: Once the wire is attached to the rail it can be fed through a 2mm hole in the baseboard ready to be connected to the main circuits.

Electrical

SKILLS GUIDE: LAYOUT CONSTRUCTION

WIRING A SECTION SWITCH

For analogue controlled layouts, switches are a great boon as they allow sections of the layout to be isolated from the main line so that locomotives can be parked while other operations continue uninterrupted.

The simplest way to add a switched section of track on a simple analogue layout is to insert an insulated rail joiner on one rail. Solder a wire to the rail either side of the insulated rail joiner then connect those wires to an on/off single pole switch. By extending the wires the

switch can be mounted in a convenient position and once you are proficient at adding switches they can be installed at locations all around a layout.

BASEBOARD CONNECTIONS ABOVE THE BOARD

If you are building a portable layout then a means of securing the ends of the rails to the baseboard will be necessary so they don't become damaged in transit. The simplest and most effective is to use copper clad sleeper which is available in strips. Alternatively DCC Concepts offers packs of pre-cut sleepers with soldering pads which offer a quick and convenient way of making baseboard joints.

To use the DCC Concepts sleepers, cut away one sleeper from the plastic web of the track either side of the baseboard joint. Drill two 1mm holes through each end either side of the rails on the DCC Concepts sleeper and pin it to the baseboard under the track. Solder the rails to the soldering pads on the sleepers and that's the job done. Repeat on both sides of the baseboard joint then cut the track. You will need a wired connection to take the power across the baseboard joint.

BASEBOARD CONNECTIONS BELOW THE BOARD

There are several options available when it comes to connecting wires between baseboards, but our preferred method is to use plug-in terminal blocks which have screw fixings to secure wires into the terminals. This method means modifications are very simple to make and that the job can be done quickly without the need for soldering. The plug-in terminal blocks are available from Rapid Electronics and Squires Tools and can be cut to length from the 12-pin strips as required.

DIAGRAM 1

Above: For analogue control, as we turn the controller from OFF to MAXIMUM the motor in the locomotive will run faster and faster. When we turn the knob back to off the motor stops. If we then change the direction switch and move the knob again the motor runs in the opposite direction.

To do this the controller puts a voltage across the two rails. This is what causes the motor to run. As the voltage increases from 0 (off) to 12 (maximum), the motor goes faster. If we change the direction switch then the voltage is applied the other way around and goes from 0 (off) to 12 (maximum) in reverse. A convention has arisen that the locomotive will move forward if the right-hand rail is positive and backwards if it is negative. This ensures that if two locomotives are being run by one controller they will both travel in the same direction.

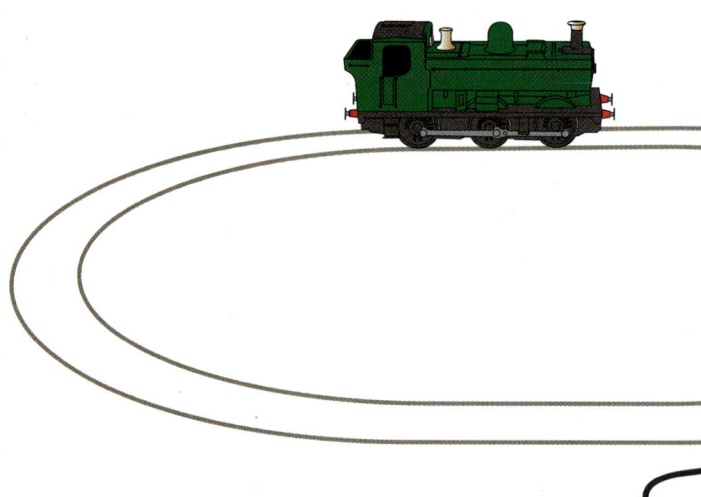

DIAGRAM 3

The problem with having two locomotives on the same track is that they both move at once and probably at different speeds. A common requirement on model railways is the ability to stop a locomotive responding to the controller. To do this we need to use a switch. These are just like light switches; they can stop the electricity flowing to part of the layout and stop any locomotives on that section responding to the controller.

Let's assume we now have two ovals of track, with a locomotive on each. Both ovals are connected to the controller and both locomotives run at the same time. If we put a switch in the red wire leading to the left-hand oval we can have both trains running if the switch is on, or just the right-hand train running if the switch is off. If we were to put another switch in the red wire leading to the right hand oval we could then choose to have either of the trains running on their own, both running at the same time or both stopped no matter how much we turn the controller.

principles

For this example of how model railway electrics work we will assume we are looking at a standard 12v DCC ready analogue locomotive; it can be any scale or gauge. Inside is an electric motor connected to the track.

DIAGRAM 2

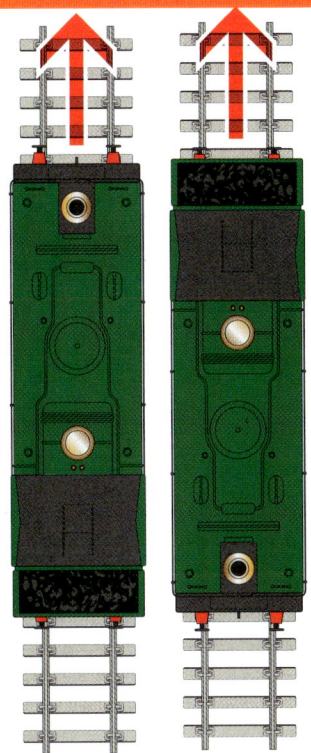

If you lift the locomotive travelling 'up the page' off the track, turn it around and replace it, it will carry on moving 'up the page'.
So if we have a controller connected to an oval of track and we put two locomotives on the track they will both run clockwise, or anti-clockwise, at the same time and at roughly similar speeds dpending on their wheel size and gearing.

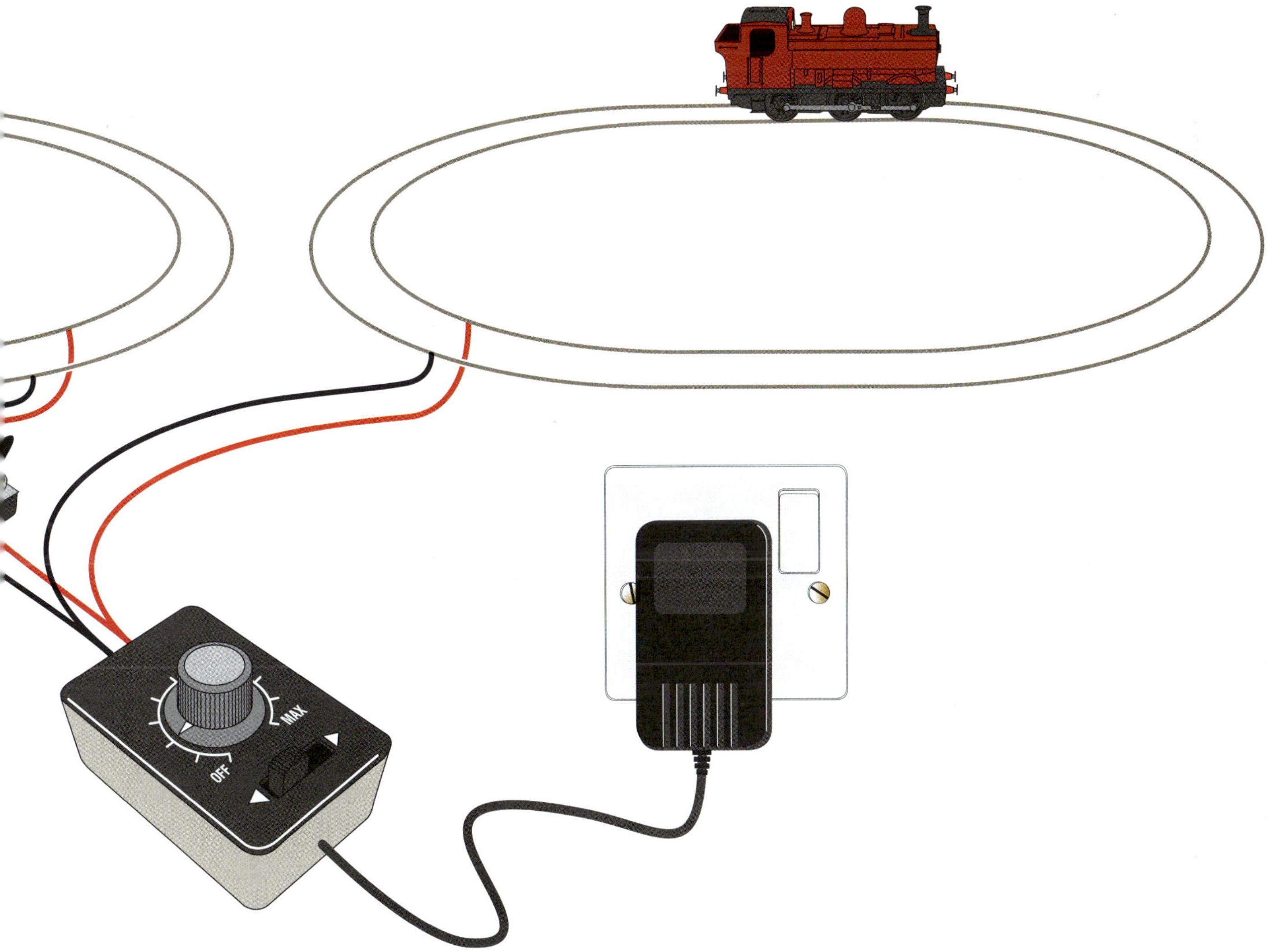

SKILLS GUIDE: LAYOUT CONSTRUCTION

Going Digital

Advances in technology and increased manufacturer take-up have seen Digital Command Control (DCC) gain significant popularity. **MARK CHIVERS** highlights just some of the benefits of going digital.

WITHOUT DOUBT, going digital introduces a new way of operating a model railway, but is the time and investment required to convert your control system and locomotives really worth it? For the *Hornby Magazine* team, the answer is a resounding YES! The flexibility to control your entire layout from one handset and ability to select your choice of locomotive without affecting others on the track at the push of a few buttons is very exciting. Factor in the options to turn lights on and off, select digital sound functions and add smoke generator effects to your locomotives as well, and you have the makings of an exhilarating and realistic experience which puts you firmly in the driving seat.

That said, it can appear quite daunting at first, not just in terms of time and finances to make the conversion from analogue control, but also in getting to grips with the terminology and technology itself. Digital Command Control (DCC) needn't be scary. If you wish to simply place a decoder into a compatible locomotive

and operate it using the pre-set default values, this is usually sufficient. However, as you become more adept and confident with your digital setup, you can begin to tweak settings known as Configuration Variables (CVs) to enhance the overall operation yet further, such as slower acceleration and deceleration rates, set the maximum speed and even alter lighting settings to suit your needs.

You can keep things as simple as you feel comfortable with and enjoy the experience of going digital by taking a methodical and considered approach to the transition. Choose a few key locomotives from your collection to convert and consider the layout's future control requirements to get you up and running. Give thought to your current track plan, as well as your aspirations for something larger and more involved in the future. This will help when it comes to sourcing a suitable Digital Command Station (controller), which are available to suit all pockets from budget handheld controllers to top-end high specification systems. Keeping things simple initially will ensure the changeover is manageable and cost-effective without breaking the bank.

Accessory decoders, like this DCC Concepts AD series board for Cobalt motors, are used to power equipment such as point motors. These sophisticated boards offer feedback for control panels as well as frog polarity switching. They are available for solenoid point motors as well.

Fundamentals

Digital operation is fundamentally different from analogue control in that the former controls the locomotive while the latter controls the track. To put this into context, analogue control relies on a user-determined Direct Current (DC) power feed to the rails, through a traditional power controller, which in turn sets a locomotive in motion. As the control throttle is increased, more power is supplied to the track enabling the locomotive to pick up speed, and vice versa. Of course, in this instance all locomotives on that section of track will move in the same direction and at a similar speed, unless you have installed isolating sections. Direction is determined by simply changing the polarity, most commonly via a switch on the controller.

Digital control takes an altogether different approach and supplies a constant Alternating Current (AC) power feed to the rails, which results in the track being permanently 'live'. Data is then transmitted from the digital power controller through the rails to a specific

Digital control allows multiple train movements to be handled through one controller and the addition of more user controlled accessories. This Heljan Gresley 'O2' 2-8-0 is fitted with a Zimo MX644 sound decoder, 'sugar cube' speaker and decoder controlled Seuthe smoke generator. It works a coal train through the station while a Bachmann Fowler 'Jinty' 0-6-0T with a Zimo 8-pin decoder shunts in the yard.

SKILLS GUIDE: LAYOUT CONSTRUCTION

DIGITAL COMMAND CONTROL

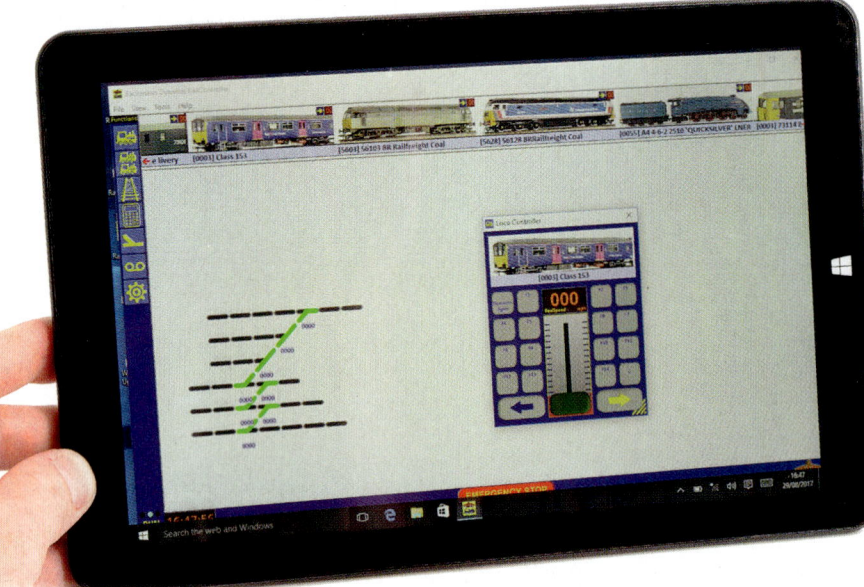

Computer control is increasing in popularity for British model railways with Bachmann and Hornby both offering their own solutions bespoke to their controllers while aftermarket suppliers, such as iTrain, have developed more flexible systems to operate with a wide range of digital controllers.

Hornby Magazine's Twelve Trees Junction uses two digital system to operate this 24ft x 10ft layout. Gaugemaster's Prodigy drives the trains allowing multiple operators to get involved while Hornby's RailMaster software connected to an Elite controller provides power and control for points and accessories on a separate feed.

onboard locomotive digital decoder which converts the data into actions, allowing the engine to move off, pick up speed, slow down or simply switch direction. Each decoder-fitted locomotive has its own unique address, which means you can have multiple locomotives sat on the same stretch of track, but only the selected locomotive will take notice of the commands.

Taking things further, you can then select additional addresses and set the models to operate at different speeds or opposing directions on the same stretch, if you like, simultaneously! This is particularly useful if you are modelling a steam or diesel locomotive depot, with multiple movements in a limited space.

The system can also be fine-tuned to suit your needs, so it is worth doing your homework and comparing specifications between systems and decoder types. For example, you will find that some locomotive decoders offer more customisation options than others through their onboard CVs which enable you to adjust individual settings to enhance running characteristics further.

Digital conversion

To make the switch to digital all you really need is a control system, a handful of decoders and a circuit of track to get you up and running. Nothing more. To convert a layout to digital operation can be as simple as swapping the two wires from the analogue controller to the replacement digital command centre. If the layout features a series of isolated section switches, these can be switched to be permanently 'live' and the layout should operate as intended.

For *Hornby Magazine's* 'OO' gauge office test layout Topley Dale, we opted for the flexibility of analogue and digital operation. Whilst this may seem at odds with the spirit of digital control, it was imperative that we maintained the flexibility so that we can test review models under analogue and digital conditions. To achieve this, we can split out one circuit for analogue control whilst also operating the other digitally. Simple plug-in terminals allow different controllers to be plugged in to each circuit, plus with matching plugs to the track feed wiring, any control system can be connected for testing purposes too.

All turnouts are controlled digitally via DCC Concepts' ADS series accessory decoders, while the layout's Dapol operating semaphore signals are linked to Train-Tech SC3 digital signal decoders. Obviously, care is required, and it is important not to leave an analogue locomotive on the digitally-controlled circuit. If this does happen, it is usually easy enough to spot as the locomotive in question will emit a buzzing sound. Extended exposure could result in damage, so remove it as quickly as possible. Conversely, you can place and operate a DCC-fitted locomotive on the analogue circuit without problem. It is also worth mentioning at this point that some DCC sound-fitted locomotives will operate with limited sound functions on analogue layouts – check individual decoders for more details.

For larger and more complex situations, additional power bus feeds and development of power districts may be worth considering in the future. There's also an extensive array of add-on equipment which can enhance operations further including power boosters, reverse loop modules, frog-juicers and more. This latter item has proved its worth on *Hornby Magazine's* 'OO' gauge BR Southern Region exhibition layout Twelve Trees Junction, as it provides effective polarity switching through the complex crossings, reducing potential

DIGITAL TERMINOLOGY	
Accessory decoder	Fixed location digital decoder that can control signals, point motors and other accessories.
Address	Identifying number for a DCC fitted locomotive or accessory decoder.
Command station	Control hub of a DCC operated layout.
Consisting	Two or more locomotives operating together using the same DCC address.
CVs	Configuration Variable. Programmable DCC decoder settings.
DCC	Digital Command Control.
DCC booster	Provides extra power rating to the track to improve DCC signals and allow more locomotives to be operated.
DCC fitted	Model supplied with a factory fitted DCC decoder.
DCC on board	Model supplied with a factory fitted DCC decoder.
DCC ready	Model supplied with a DCC decoder socket only and no decoder.
Decoder	Printed circuit board for operating model railway locomotives and accessories.
Function output	Used to control functions and features on DCC fitted locomotive or carriages such as lights and sounds.
Main track	DCC term for operational railway layout.
Power bus	DCC layout power supply cable with dropper wires feeding the track at regular intervals.
Programming track	DCC term for track which is separate from the main line for programming locomotive CVs.
Route setting	Series of points operating together to form a defined route on a layout.
Speed steps	DCC power control increments. The more steps you have, the smoother the speed transition. Equally divided into 14, 28 and 128 steps depending on controller setting.

DIGITAL COMMAND CONTROL

10 top tips
GOING DIGITAL

1. Keep things simple and move one step at a time

2. Read product reviews, check their purpose and the experience of others before buying

3. When choosing a controller try different types in a shop before committing to a purchase

4. Analogue and digital can be used on the same layout, but they MUST be kept separate

5. Choose a simple locomotive as your first DCC installation project – 21-pin socket models are easiest

6. Set yourself attainable goals in upgrading a locomotive fleet to digital – doing it 'overnight' will be expensive

7. Plan out an addressing system early – we use the last four digits from each locomotive number as their address - we can't forget them that way

8. When adding accessory decoders select number ranges for certain aspects. For example, on Topley Dale all the points are numbered in the 1-10 range while the signals are numbered in the 20-25 range

9. If you have a big layout consider keeping analogue control for one circuit and introducing DCC control for another

10. Enjoy it! Digital control brings a whole new world of operation to model railways

short-circuit issues. Research is key here and visiting retailers such as Digitrains with specialist knowledge is well worth while.

Control options are varied and designed to suit all pockets, ranging from entry-level and mid-range examples to advanced systems such as ESU's ECoS command station (Cat No: 50220) which comes with 6 Amp output, full colour touch-screen display, dual controllers and built-in booster. No matter which option you choose, at the very least you will enjoy refined throttle control with the ability to control multiple sound functions, turnouts, signals, double-headed consists and more.

Some systems, such as Hornby's RailMaster and Bachmann's Dynamis RailController software packages, introduce a certain degree of automation into the equation too, offering the spectacle of trains operating remotely on some sections of a layout, whilst close control can be maintained in other areas.

Options

Manufacturers have certainly embraced digital provision in recent times with a rolling programme of chassis upgrades to older models and inclusion of integrated circuitry to newly-tooled models. Most new locomotives and multiple come ready for digital conversion – usually as simple as plugging the pins of a newly-purchased digital decoder into the onboard decoder socket. Look for symbols and descriptions on boxes that refer to the model as 'DCC ready'.

Other options include DCC fitted/DCC onboard models, which come with a pre-installed DCC decoder and DCC sound-fitted models come with a digital sound decoder

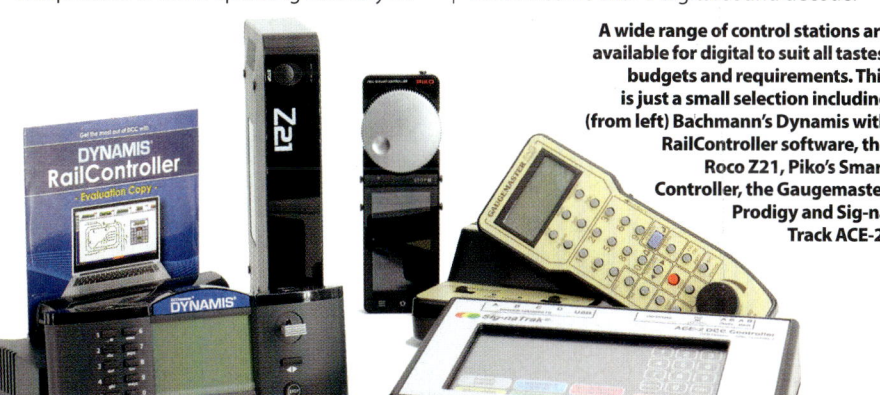

A wide range of control stations are available for digital to suit all tastes, budgets and requirements. This is just a small selection including (from left) Bachmann's Dynamis with RailController software, the Roco Z21, Piko's Smart Controller, the Gaugemaster Prodigy and Sig-na Track ACE-2.

SKILLS GUIDE: LAYOUT CONSTRUCTION

DIGITAL COMMAND CONTROL

Even the smallest of locomotives are equipped with decoder sockets today, but careful selection of the decoder type to be installed will be required to ensure that it will fit. This is Hornby's Wainwright 'H' 0-4-4T which has an 8-pin decoder socket mounted in the firebox area.

New production models are fitted with decoder sockets and many now have provision for installation of a speaker too. This is a Hornby air-smoothed 'West Country' equipped with a Zimo MX645 decoder, a 28mm square 3D printed speaker and a single 'stay alive' capacitor in the tender.

and speaker already fitted. Manufacturers often factor in enclosures for digital speaker mounts too, aiding those wishing to make their own digital sound installations.

Before installing a decoder, you will need to identify what type of socket is fitted to your new model. Options include 6-pin, 8-pin, Next18 and 21-pin decoder sockets, depending on the manufacturer, model, size and available space.

6-pin and Next18 sockets are usually used in 'N' gauge and smaller 'OO' gauge locomotives. Bachmann's recent 'OO' gauge releases have featured 21-pin decoder sockets, as have Dapol and Heljan's most recent 'OO' products, while Hornby opts for 8-pin decoder sockets as standard for most of its DCC ready locomotives and its Twin Track Sound (TTS) sound-fitted models. Before purchasing decoders, it is certainly worth double-checking the pin type required.

For older models and those that have yet to receive a DCC decoder socket upgrade, it is possible to hardwire a decoder by soldering the relevant wires to a suitable plain harness-style decoder, although some older models, for example, Mainline models with split-chassis, can present a major challenge.

Once installed, the decoder will control the locomotive's motor and onboard light functions (if included). Decoders range from basic two-function examples which offer motor control plus two lighting function outputs, for example, to high-end digital sound specimens with the capability to control the motor, sound functions, speaker, lights, a smoke generator, 'stay alive' capacitors and more.

A wide range of specialist products are available for digital including Train-Tech's SC3 signal controller which is designed specifically to operate Dapol semaphore signals.

Bear in mind that the more sophisticated the model in terms of lighting options, such as Dapol's 'OO' gauge Class 68 diesel locomotive, the more functions that will be required to operate them adequately. Whilst Bachmann, Dapol and Hornby retail digital decoders, further compatible options are also available from the likes of DCC Concepts, ESU, Gaugemaster, Lenz, TCS, Zimo and more. Some examples come with 'stay alive' capability, which means that they can overcome a short break in electrical continuity, with the motor appearing to continue without interruption.

Digital sound decoders make a world of difference and sound files are available for a wide range of steam, diesel and electric locomotives and multiple units. Most major manufacturers now offer versions with factory-fitted DCC sound installations. You can also install digital sound yourself with an extensive selection of UK diesel and steam projects available through specialist retailers including Coastal DCC, DC Kits/Legomanbiffo, Digitrains, Howes, Locoman Sounds, Rail Exclusive, South West Digital, YouChoos and more. Utilising ESU and Zimo digital sound decoders, these projects offer impressive functionality, realistic sound reproduction and smooth motor control for around £90-£120 per project. Most recently, Hornby has introduced its range of budget Twin Track Sound (TTS) digital sound decoders as standalone items for customer fitment, and at just over £40 each they represent a cost-effective method of adding digital sound to a fleet.

So much more

However, DCC it is not just about locomotive control as it also offers the capability to operate a wide range of accessories including turnouts, signals and lighting as

These are the main track connections on *Hornby Magazine's* 'N' gauge test track which can be operated with analogue control or digital control on the outer circuits. Simply unplugging one of the plugs and replacing it with an analogue controller takes care of the changeover. Digital and analogue must never be connected to the same circuit.

Digital control can be used outside of the lineside fence to operate accessories such as these level crossing lights developed by Train-Tech.

USEFUL LINKS	
Bachmann	www.bachmann.co.uk
Coastal DCC	www.coastaldcc.co.uk
Dapol	www.dapol.co.uk
DC Kits	www.dckits-devideos.co.uk
DCC Concepts	www.dccconcepts.com
Digitrains	www.digitrains.co.uk
ESU	www.esu.eu
Gaugemaster (Roco & Train-Tech)	www.gaugemaster.com
Heljan	www.heljan.co.uk
Hornby	www.hornby.com
Howes	www.howesmodels.co.uk
Lenz	www.digital-plus.de
Locoman Sounds	www.locomansounds.com
Rail Exclusive	www.railexclusive.com
South West Digital	www.southwestdigital.co.uk
TCS	www.tcsdcc.com
YouChoos	www.youchoos.co.uk
Zimo	www.zimo.at

DIGITAL COMMAND CONTROL

well as introducing levels of automation and train detection, to enhance operations even further. If you wish to add a special lighting effect, with a few tweaks to settings, this is also possible.

Train-Tech, now part of the Gaugemaster family, offers extensive range of model railway accessories includes buffer stop lights, colour light signals, operating level crossing lights, traffic lights and a series of lighting effect controllers offering log fire, welding and alternative flashing effects – all of which can be operated digitally. Incidentally, Train-Tech's One Touch system does most of the hard work for you at the programming stage. Just select an accessory address, press the learn button and the digital setup process is done.

Meanwhile, DCC Concept's range of station and street lighting comprises classic and modern styles which can also be optimised for digital operation, along with digitally controlled end of train lights, illuminated carriage table lamps, ground signals and much more. Its range of accessory decoders, digital point motors and DCC equipment is extensive too.

Some command centres can also be connected to desktop PCs or laptops through software such as Bachmann's *RailController* and Hornby's *RailMaster* programmes to create even more elaborate set-ups with on-screen mimic diagrams and touch-screen control. Additional third-party software such as *TrainController*, *RocRail* and *JMRI* can also be utilised to introduce further levels of sophistication to your digital setup in due course. For *Hornby Magazine's* 'OO' gauge Grosvenor Square and Twelve Trees Junction exhibition layouts, we've devised a setup which utilises two digital systems, suitably separated, to create a flexible user-friendly means of control. Whilst retaining Gaugemaster's Prodigy Advance system for locomotive control, we use Hornby's *RailMaster* control software (connected to Hornby's Elite DCC command centre) to provide an operational twin-screen schematic diagram of the layout, used purely for operating turnouts and accessories. This not only provides the added flexibility of reliable point operation on a separate circuit, it also looks the part and attracts many positive comments at exhibitions.

Further technology is available in the form of downloadable mobile applications, turning your mobile device into a handheld DCC controller with full access to function keys and on-screen mimic diagrams, which again adds a new dimension to layout control. This, though, is just a taste of the future, but factor in the ability to control points, signalling, lighting and DCC sound – all from the palm of your hand – and you have a digital experience that is both enthralling and exciting.

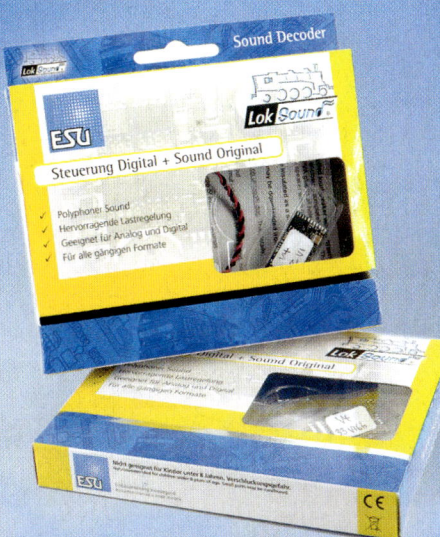

Locomotive sound decoders are available from a number of manufacturers including ESU and Zimo which can have specific sound files loaded onto them by specialist suppliers. This pair of ESU decoders were prepared by DC Kits to add realistic sound into a Class 33/1 and 4-TC combination.

With no limit to its potential and rapid advances in technology, rest assured *Hornby Magazine* will continue to embrace digital control, helping you make the most of this fascinating sector of the hobby. ■

With analogue control a section switch would be needed to isolate the Class 73 in the loop, but with digital both the 33 and 73 can be controlled independently allowing more realistic train movements.

SKILLS GUIDE: LAYOUT CONSTRUCTION

Track PLANNING

Whatever grand plan you may have for your model railway, it is likely there will be elements of compromise along the way as you hone the design. **MARK CHIVERS** offers a few track planning tips to get you started along with examples for 'OO' gauge.

HAVING IDENTIFIED the space available for a layout, it's not a good idea to start buying track and then hoping for the best. Developing a track plan really is the best way forward.

Firstly, map out your intended design - a simple pencil drawing should suffice. It will act as an indicator of the track layout and any features you may wish to include.

Consider whether it is to be a continuous loop or end-to-end scheme and if it is to be of freelance design or something based on a prototype location. You might wish to mix and match, with the option to run trains around the loops while shuttling others back and forth on a branch line or perhaps shunting to and from a yard or carriage sidings. If you are basing your layout on a prototypical location, get a feel for the area in question by tracking down relevant books and photographs to ascertain placement of structures in relation to the full-size track layout.

What follows focusses primarily on 'OO' gauge but everything is transferable to other scales.

Freelance design

You may decide to keep the layout's origins fluid, and in this case it will naturally evolve as you develop the plan, but you will still need to consider the main ingredients. These may include a station, goods yard, locomotive depot, junction, elevated section, branch line, tunnel, sidings, bridges, viaducts, a river, townscape and more.

However, it will soon become apparent that unless you have unlimited space, some elements of selective compression may be necessary such as reducing platform length or the number of sidings that will fit. Signal placement may also need to be closer together, while curves may inevitably end up much sharper than the real thing. Pointwork will almost certainly need reviewing too. Also, don't be tempted to fill all the baseboards with track – allow room for a few buildings, structures and scenery such as greenery and trees as well.

Be realistic in your aspirations and consider train lengths. When planning platform run-round loops, headshunts and stabling sidings, allow enough space for the longest locomotive in your fleet. In similar vein, multiply the length of your longest carriages accordingly to accommodate the required length in platforms. Given that a 'OO' gauge BR Mk 1 carriage measures approximately 280mm, a platform length of around 1,400mm (4ft 6in) should be considered to hold a four-coach train plus locomotive. Also,

Model railway design is about much more than just filling a baseboard with track. For the best in realism the railway needs to become part of a scene as here at Shortley Bridge station where allotments border the goods yard and station where a Class 17 Bo-Bo diesel is waiting to enter the yard to collect wagons.

consider any overhang and clearance issues that may occur on run-round loops and curves.

For multi-level layouts, ensure you allow as much of a run as possible for a gentle gradient. Realistically, a 1-in-30 gradient (a rise of 1mm over a 30mm run) is probably the steepest gradient you would wish to consider, with anything gentler being more acceptable to prevent traction issues. To help, there are off-the-shelf products available such as Woodland Scenics' Sub Terrain incline risers which come in a selection of grades and Hornby's inclined piers pack (R658) which includes seven graduated piers for use over a defined length. Again, the distance required needs to be planned into your diagram.

Track choices

Next, decide on whether you want sectional or flexible track. Code 100 sectional track is supplied with most 'OO' gauge train sets with options available from Bachmann, Hornby and Peco. It is designed to follow specific geometry to make planning simpler, with curved track pieces available in first, second, third and fourth radius options.

As the radius increases, so does the space required to form a 180-degree curve. First radius generally requiring a 742mm (2ft 4in) space, a second radius curve 876mm (2ft 9in), third radius 1,010mm (3ft 3in) and fourth radius 1,144mm (3ft 7.5in), which gives a rough indicator as to how much baseboard space to allow. Each radius can be spaced equally (67mm over centre lines) to form neat multiple curves without clearance issues, while track pieces are available in a range of sizes and arcs to suit individual needs. It is also worth bearing in mind that unless you are only running short wheelbase locomotives, most manufacturers recommend use of second radius curves and above, while the selection of turnouts available is limited.

Peco also offers an alternative track system with its Streamline range which incorporates 914mm (1yd) lengths of flexible track, together with a broader selection of turnouts in both Code 100 and Code 75 rails. This flexible track can be formed to produce bespoke flowing curves without reliance on specific geometry, as well as straight and gently curving orientations.

Pointwork includes small, medium, large and curved variants, catch points, three-way points, double-slip crossings, Y points and more. The added benefit to the flexible track range is that it can be gently bent to shape, cut to length and is more cost-effective.

One of the issues traditional Code 100 or 75 track is that the sleeper size and spacing are not prototypical. Therefore, a range of manufacturers - C&L, DCC Concepts, Peco and SMP for example - offer finescale 'OO' flexible track with more accurate sleepers and rails. Peco now offers a range of complementary turnouts and crossing under its Bullhead range.

Planning applications

Having taken these factors into consideration, as the plan develops you will find that a detailed and accurate representation will reap benefits. Over and above the simple pencil drawing on graph paper, there are numerous options that can be utilised to help the process. Computer based track planning software is available to download including options from AnyRail, Hornby Trackmaster, SCARM, XTrackCAD and WinRail. Each offers libraries of track parts to gradually build up your plan. We've used the SCARM software to design the trackplans which start on the next page. One bonus of SCARM is that you can also view the finished design in 3D form too, which is very useful. 'Scene blocking', how you disguise the exits to the fiddleyards, is an important part of designing a layout.

Traditional methods are also available including Peco's downloadable turnout templates which can be placed directly on the baseboard so you can draw the design directly onto it.

An additional tip when plotting your plan is to include scale representations of the baseboard sections too as these will help with turnout placement. If the layout is likely to be semi-portable, try to keep points away from joints between baseboards and any strengthening battens below, as these may cause issues if you wish to place point motors beneath the surface.

There are also numerous planning books and websites available. Or let the five superb track plans we've already prepared for you (starting on the next page) fire your imagination! ∎

USEFUL LINKS	
Manufacturer	Website
Anyrail	www.anyrail.com
Bachmann	www.bachmann.co.uk
C&L Finescale	www.finescale.org.uk
DCC Concepts	www.dccconcepts.com
Hornby	www.hornby.com
Peco	www.peco-uk.com
SCARM	www.scarm.info
Scale Model Products	www.marcway.net
WinRail	www.winrail.com
XTrackCAD	www.xtrkcad.org

SKILLS GUIDE: LAYOUT CONSTRUCTION

TRACKPLANS

IF SPACE IS LIMITED, a small baseboard may be the answer. Plan A measures just 4ft x 18in and aims to represent a small country halt with adjacent goods yard and locomotive shed. Whilst small, it packs a lot into the available space with single face station platform, small headshunt, run-round loop, locomotive shed, goods platform and goods shed. Ideal as a shunting puzzle layout, it comprises two space-saving Peco double-slip crossings (Cat No. SL-E190), two medium left-hand (SL-E196) and two medium right-hand points (SL-E195), together with five lengths of flexible track (SL-100F).

Access to and from the layout is via off-scene cassette storage to the top left of the scheme, with provision for a two-carriage passenger train at the station platform, while the run-round loop could also be used for shunting goods trains too. Whilst the train locomotive heads to the shed, the resident shunting locomotive can distribute the wagons accordingly and reform the train for its return journey, making for some interesting operating sequences, despite its diminutive size.

WHAT WE USED

Product	Manufacturer	Cat No.	Quantity
Flexible track, yard length	Peco	SL-100F	5
Double slip crossing	Peco	SL-E190	2
Medium radius right-hand point	Peco	SL-E195	1
Medium radius left-hand point	Peco	SL-E196	2

KEY

1. Station halt
2. Platform
3. Station halt shelter
4. Fence
5. Signalbox
6. Locomotive shed
7. Water tower
8. Goods platform
9. Goods shed
10. Goods yard
11. Wall
12. Gardens
13. Terrace houses
14. Coaling stage
15. To/from cassette yard

● For more compact layout plans see HM117, March 2017.

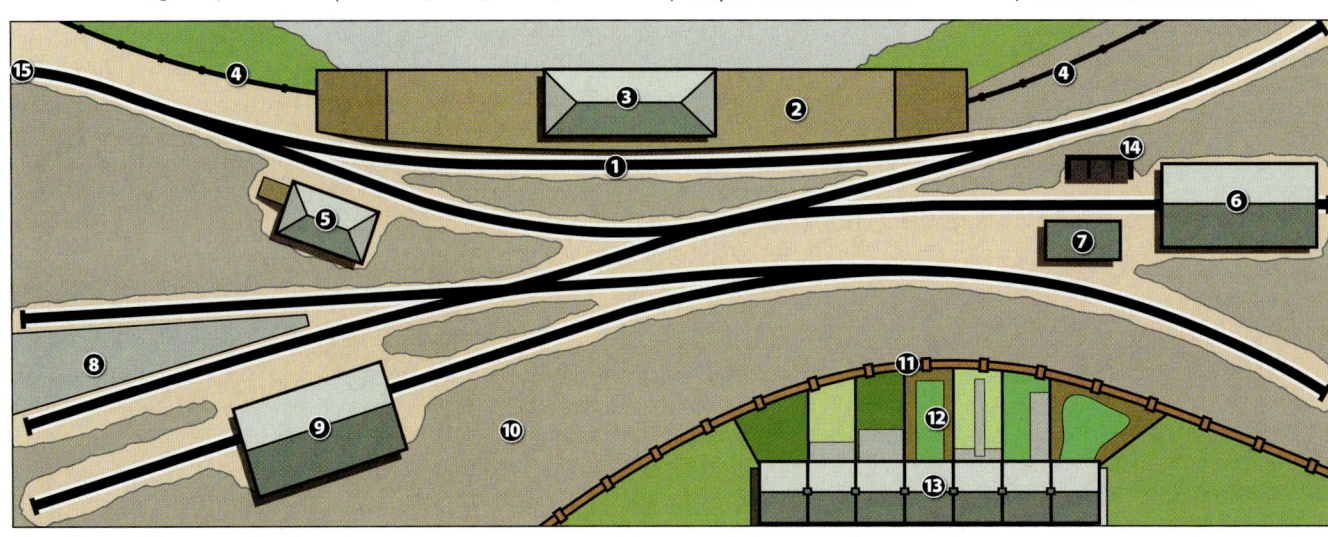

PLAN B is an end-to-end design that represents a coastal passenger terminus, in this case at a West Country location, where it is assumed summer holiday traffic makes extensive use of the double-faced station platform and accompanying carriage sidings. As there are no run-round facilities as such, locomotive hauled services would require shunt-releasing – this means that a station pilot would couple onto the rear of an arriving train to take the carriages away. The train engine can then reverse along the platform to head to the depot.

This manoeuvre will take the carriages through the complicated double-slip crossing at the centre of the scheme and then see them propelled into one of the carriage sidings. Meanwhile the locomotive could head to the small locomotive servicing facility for turning, as well as replenishing with water and coal ready for its next working. A goods yard is included too, with direct access to/from the locomotive shed to reduce conflicting movements with passenger arrivals and departures.

At 14ft x 3ft, the scenic area for this layout utilises Peco Code 100 Setrack and Streamline track components and would suit a large shed or garage, as the hidden storage yards would require additional space to hold suitably lengthy passenger and goods trains while 'off-scene'. The storage yard design could involve a return loop if you have space, a series of dead end sidings, a traverser or cassettes.

● For more coastal layout plans see HM110, August 2016.

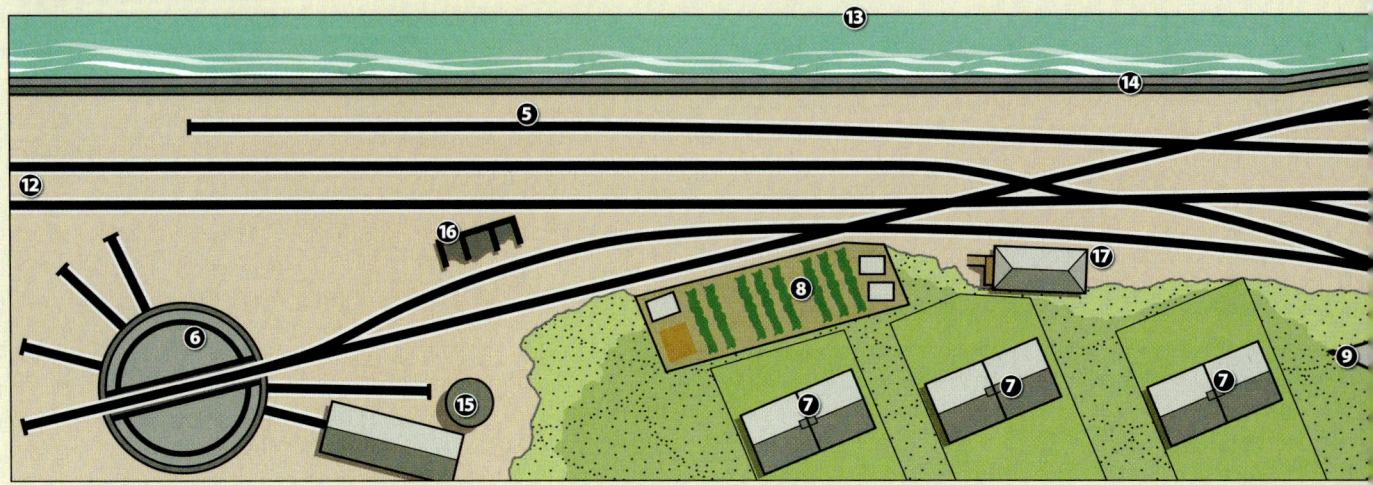

TRACKPLANS

www.keymodelworld.com

WHAT WE USED

Product	Manufacturer	Cat No.	Quantity
Turntable kit	Peco	LK-55	1
Flexible track, yard length	Peco	SL-100F	14
Medium radius right-hand point	Peco	SL-E195	3
Medium radius left-hand point	Peco	SL-E196	2

KEY

1. Servicing shed
2. Turntable
3. Maintenance shed/offices
4. Hoist gantry
5. Fuel tanks
6. Stores
7. Crew room
8. Shunters mess
9. Secure compound for flammable liquids
10. Inspection shed
11. Hidden sidings
12. Grounded van body (sand store)

THIS SCHEME is altogether different in that it portrays a diesel-era locomotive depot with an operating turntable dominating the scene. Ideal for displaying your locomotive fleet at its best, there are nine stabling roads, plus offshoots to other areas of the depot including the maintenance shed, inspection shed and further stabling sidings. Access to the turntable is through the two-road servicing/fuelling shed, with the entrance/exit to the layout at the right-hand side. Again, this would require a separate off-scene storage yard or cassette storage system. Two hidden sidings are also provided at the top of the scheme, which could also be used to change motive power and feed them in and out of the layout. At 8ft x 3ft, this plan utilises three Peco Code 75 medium right-hand (SL-E195) and two medium left-hand turnouts (SL-E196), together with 14 lengths of flexible track (SL-100F). Extra detailing can be added with hoist gantries, office buildings, fuel storage tanks and more to create some exciting scenarios as locomotives progress through the depot, ready to be stabled.

Whilst primarily intended as a diesel era layout, it wouldn't take a lot of effort to backdate it to the steam era too.

● **For more depot layout plans see HM101, November 2015 and HM125, November 2017.**

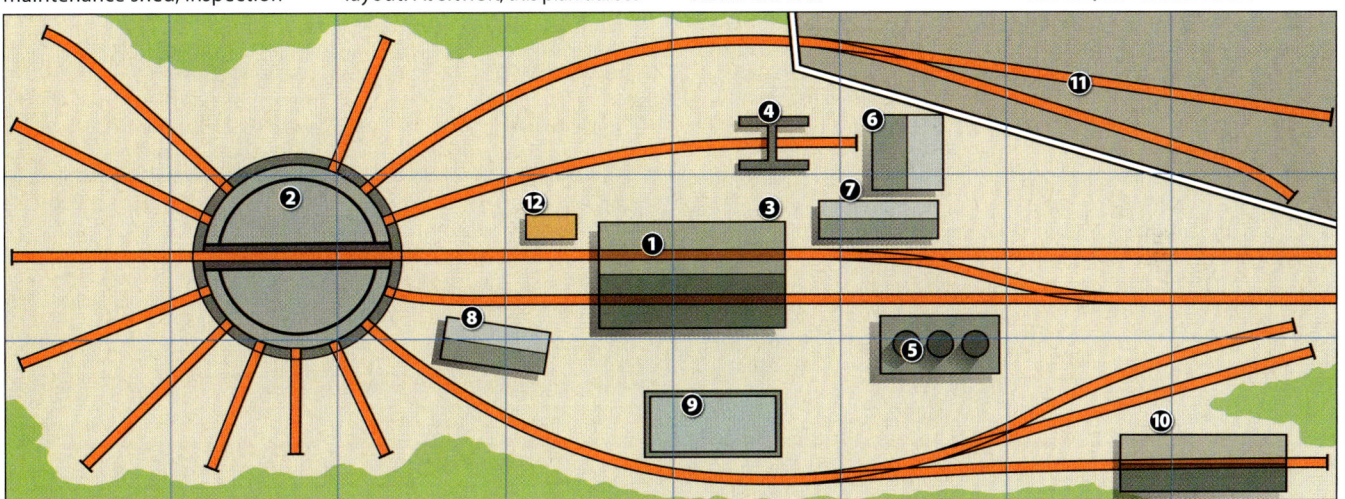

KEY

1. Platform
2. Station building
3. Goods shed
4. Carriage sidings
5. Carriage siding headshunt
6. Turntable
7. Houses/gardens
8. Allotments
9. Fence
10. Goods office
11. Goods yard area
12. To/from storage yard
13. Sea
14. Sea wall
15. Engine shed/water tower
16. Coaling stage
17. Signalbox
18. Sidings

The Great Western Main Line's sea wall through Dawlish and on to Teignmouth is probably the best known of all Britain's coastal railway lines. On August 6 1976 1068 *Western Reliance* approaches Teignmouth with a Down West of England express. Graham Smith/Railphotoprints.co.uk.

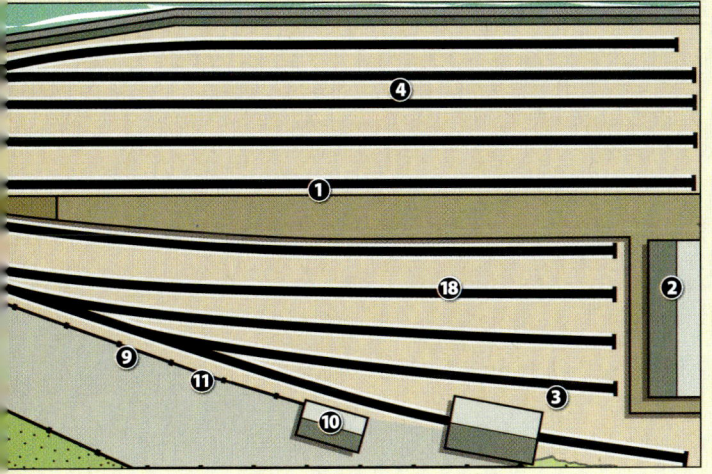

WHAT WE USED

Product	Manufacturer	Cat No.	Quantity
Turntable kit	Peco	LK-55	1
Flexible track, yard length	Peco	SL-100	24
Double-slip crossing	Peco	SL-90	5
Medium radius right hand point	Peco	SL-95	3
Medium radius left hand point	Peco	SL-96	3
Double straight	Peco	ST-201	3
Short straight	Peco	ST-202	1
Long straight	Peco	ST-204	1
Medium crossing	Peco	ST-250	1

SKILLS GUIDE: LAYOUT CONSTRUCTION

PLAN D

Rebuilt Bulleid 'Battle of Britain' 4-6-2 34090 *Sir Eustace Missenden* crosses Battledown flyover at Worting with a Weymouth-Waterloo working on May 30 1964.
Hugh Ballantyne/Railphotoprints.co.uk.

PLAN D IS DIFFERENT in that not only is it a continuous loop plan, it also doesn't feature a station. The track plan measures 16ft x 12ft and includes two multi-level junctions – one at the top and the other at the bottom of the scheme. Each junction features a representation of the prototype, although clearly a full-scale replica would be impossible to reproduce in the space available. A novel twist with this design is that the lower level lines that pass beneath the junction at the top of the plan become the elevated lines at the other junction, and vice versa. As a result, consideration is required to the rise and fall of the lines to allow sufficient clearance beneath each of the flyovers – especially amongst the four lines to the far right of the plan.

Allowance for a 7ft run between junctions is required, possibly more for gradual gradients. In addition to the main circuits, storage lines are also included within the centre of the scheme, with enough stabling for multiple train formations, accessible from the inner circuit. One road could be kept clear to enable trains to divert off the main lines and so lengthen the journey time.

Ideal for a garage, shed or loft conversion, if you just want to run trains, this layout could prove ideal, with ample space to loop trains off the main line and create exciting scenarios. With a longer room the layout could be extended for more realistic gradients.

● For more junction layout plans see HM123, September 2017.

WHAT WE USED

Product	Manufacturer	Cat No.	Quantity
Flexible track, yard length	Peco	SL-100F	85
Curved double radius right point	Peco	SL-E186	4
Curved double radius left point	Peco	SL-E187	5
Large radius left point	Peco	SL-E189	1
Medium radius right point	Peco	SL-E195	5
Medium radius left point	Peco	SL-E196	4
Large radius 'Y' point	Peco	SL-E198	3

PLAN E

The trackwork at Barnstaple Junction's station approaches offer superb modelling potential, as shown in Plan C. Bulleid 'Battle of Britain' 34061 *73 Squadron* eases through the junction with the 3pm from Ilfracombe on May 19 1959.
Ken Cook/Rail Archive Stephenson.

OUR FINAL PLAN represents a traditional continuous loop track diagram with a large station and a distinctive junction at one end of the station offering an eye-catching spectacle. Provision is also included for a link to further 'off-scene' storage or additional loops – perhaps even another end-to-end station plan – for added potential in the future if you have the space. With three main platform faces, plus a bay platform, there is plenty of scope for passenger operations while parcels and branch line trains could also be operated. In the lower section of the scheme, five storage roads with two extra kick-back sidings are provided, although more could be added if space allows.

At 12ft x 8ft, this plan would suit a large spare room, garage, loft conversion or shed. Station platforms, as drawn, could accommodate three or four carriage trains and may be extended if you have room, particularly if located in a loft space.

The plan requires 25 turnouts, with two different sized crossovers to achieve the distinctive angles, including three short crossings (SL-E193), one long crossing (SL-E194), one double-slip crossing (SL-E190), 11 curved double radius points (SL-E186/E187) and four large radius turnouts (SL-E188/E189). The remainder is made up of medium radius turnouts (SL-E195/E196) in the station area, plus a single small radius Y point to get the angle just right for the short crossings at the top of the plan.

With long-distance and branch line passenger trains, pick-up goods and milk traffic potential, it offers plenty of operational scope.

● For more secondary station layout plans see HM103, January 2016.

WHAT WE USED

Product	Manufacturer	Cat No.	Quantity
Flexible track, yard length	Peco	SL-100F	40
Curved double radius right-hand point	Peco	SL-E186	5
Curved double radius left-hand point	Peco	SL-E187	6
Large radius right-hand point	Peco	SL-E188	3
Large radius left-hand point	Peco	SL-E189	1
Short crossing	Peco	SL-E193	3
Long crossing	Peco	SL-E194	1
Double-slip crossing	Peco	SL-E190	1
Medium radius right-hand point	Peco	SL-E195	2
Medium radius left-hand point	Peco	SL-E196	1
Small radius Y point	Peco	SL-E197	1

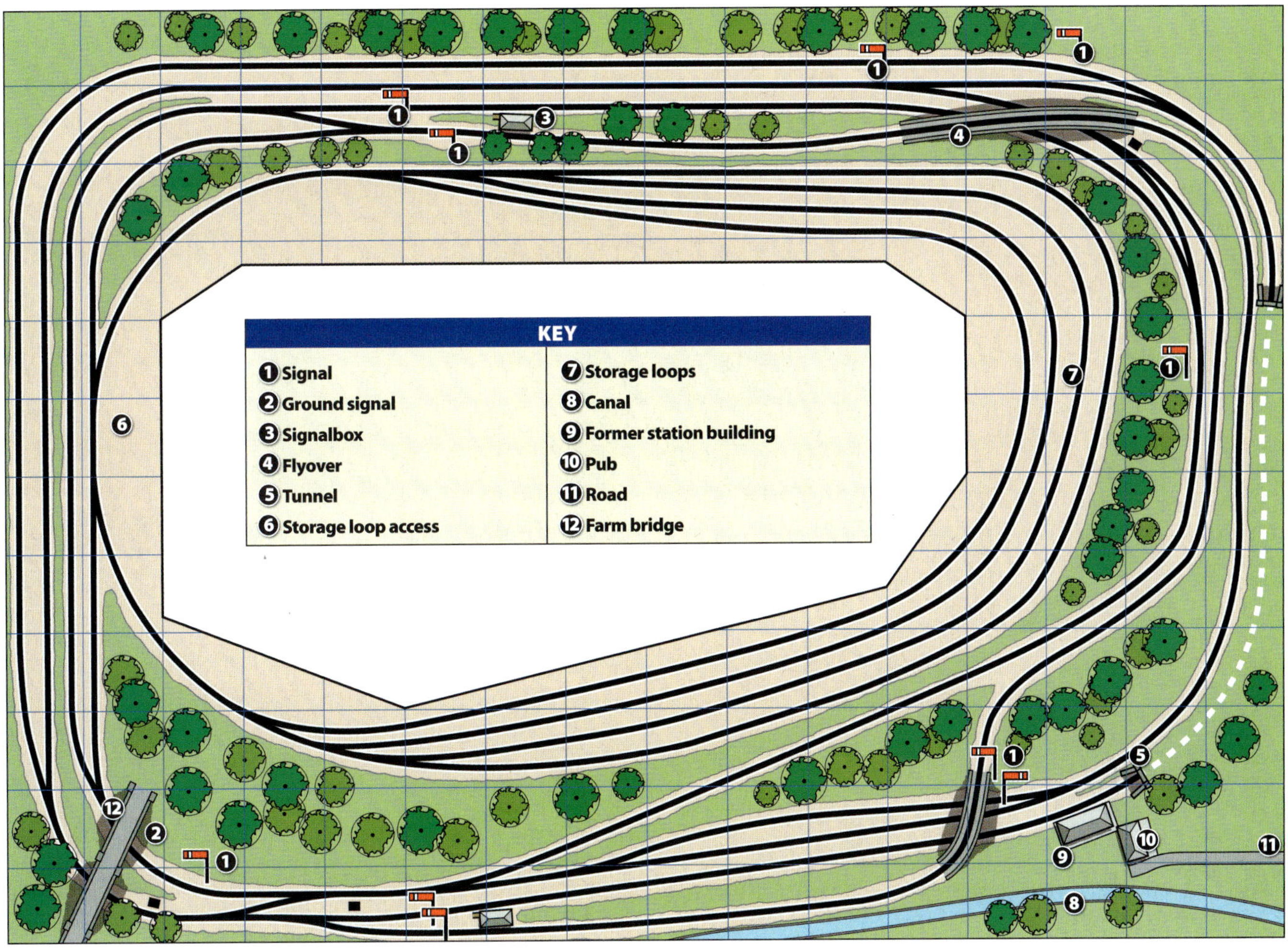

TRACKPLANS

KEY	
① Signal	⑦ Storage loops
② Ground signal	⑧ Canal
③ Signalbox	⑨ Former station building
④ Flyover	⑩ Pub
⑤ Tunnel	⑪ Road
⑥ Storage loop access	⑫ Farm bridge

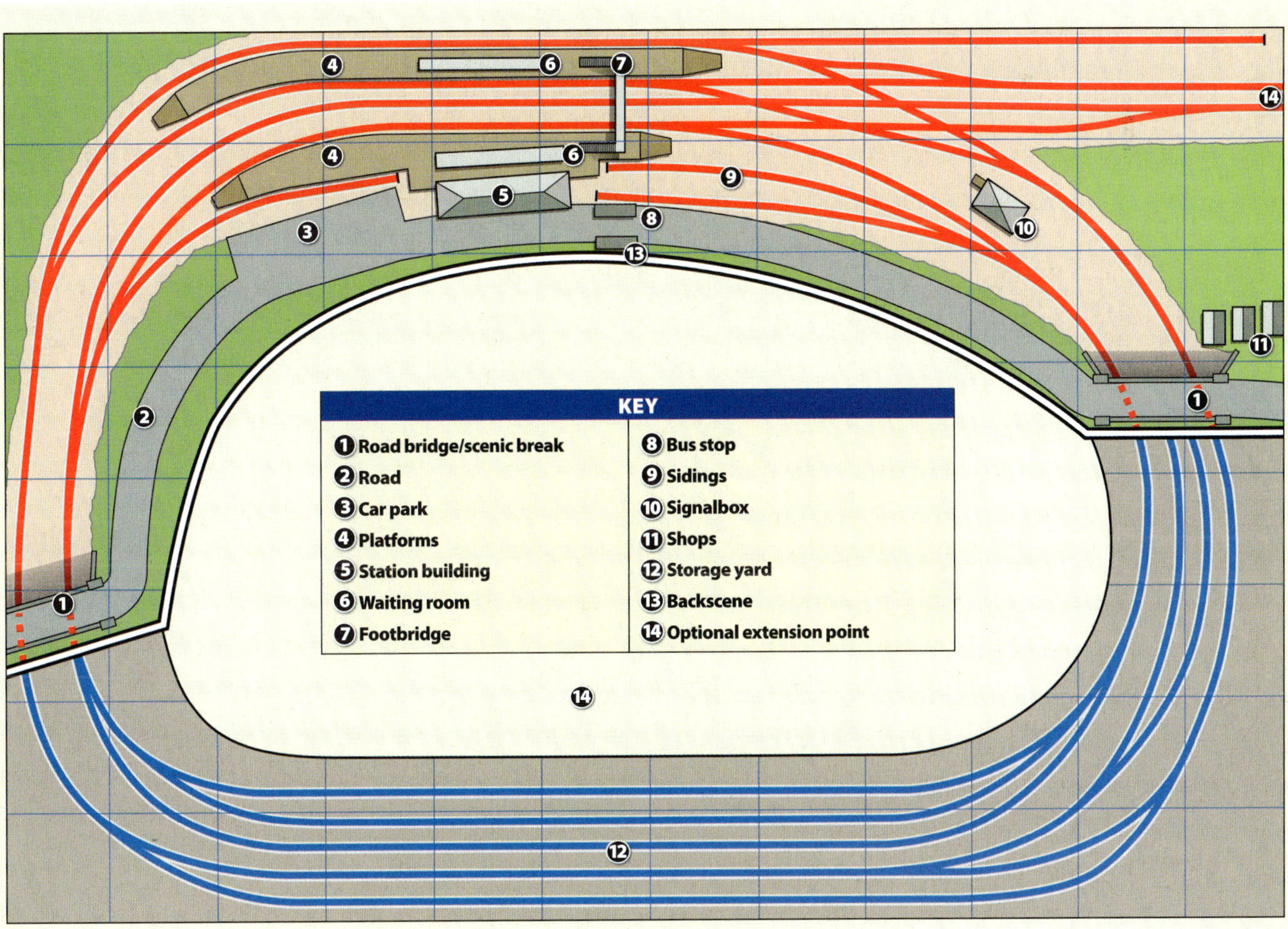

KEY	
① Road bridge/scenic break	⑧ Bus stop
② Road	⑨ Sidings
③ Car park	⑩ Signalbox
④ Platforms	⑪ Shops
⑤ Station building	⑫ Storage yard
⑥ Waiting room	⑬ Backscene
⑦ Footbridge	⑭ Optional extension point

SKILLS GUIDE: LAYOUT CONSTRUCTION

Bachmann's new 'OO9' Double Fairlie 0-4-4-0T was the catalyst for a new narrow gauge layout project in the workshop. Here the new arrival passes the slate sidings with a passenger working. Scenery is coming next.

A Fairlie Good Idea (Fairlie Syniad Da)

The arrival of Bachmann's new 'OO9' Double Fairlie 0-4-4-0T put **MIKE WILD'S** modelling mind into overdrive resulting in a new project entering the works with a Ffestiniog theme.

What happens when a brand new locomotive arrives that we weren't expecting? Ideas spring to mind and new layout designs start swirling. And that's exactly what happened the day that Bachmann's all-new model of the Ffestiniog Railway Double Fairlie arrived in the Hornby Magazine office for review.

To be perfectly honest, a new layout plan wasn't on the horizon at the beginning of November. Having just brought our Great Central Railway themed layout up to an exhibition ready standard (although far from finished) it was time for a break from layouts. However, we only have a simple out and back narrow gauge layout available and it is quite restricted in the scenes that it has to offer, so it didn't take too long to send my planning mind into overdrive and come up with an idea following arrival of Earl of Merioneth.

The plan for this project is to create a simple layout which won't take long to build. In terms of hours, I was thinking along the lines of three working days total to get the full layout assembled, running and the basic scenery laid out so that it looked the part with trains running. Naturally there would be more detail to add in the future, but there is no need to rush that element of a build.

The baseboard size was quickly established at 8ft x 2ft 6in which allowed a reasonable running length in 'OO9' and the opportunity to introduce a continuous run scene. Building on the success of the GCR layout which didn't have an off-scene storage yard, the aim was another multi-sided design and that meant it could incorporate a station scene, engine shed, main line running plus a shunting yard for slate wagons.

Orders were promptly placed for the track and with the support of Bachmann's Scenecraft arm we had all the buildings to hand that we needed to get off the ground. Next came a trip to the local timber merchant to collect a sheet of 9mm plywood (pre-cut with their bench saw to the right sizes for the two 4ft x 2ft 6in baseboards) together with a supporting cast of 70mm x 15mm planed timber for the baseboard frames and 44mm x 44mm planed timber for the legs.

Rapid start

Baseboard construction was the first task and follows a tried and tested method for creation of solid and reliable boards. The 9mm plywood top provides ample support for the lightweight narrow gauge trains which will be running on the layout while the frame underneath consists of two long sides, two ends and two cross-members.

Each of the boards is assembled with PVA glue followed by 4.0 x 30mm twin thread wood screws for fixing the plywood to the frame while the joints at the corners of the frame were made with slightly longer 4.0 x 35mm wood screws through 2.5mm pilot holes to prevent the ends of the timbers splitting. You can see the full step by step guide for our baseboards in the Beginner's Guide to Layout Construction supplement with this issue.

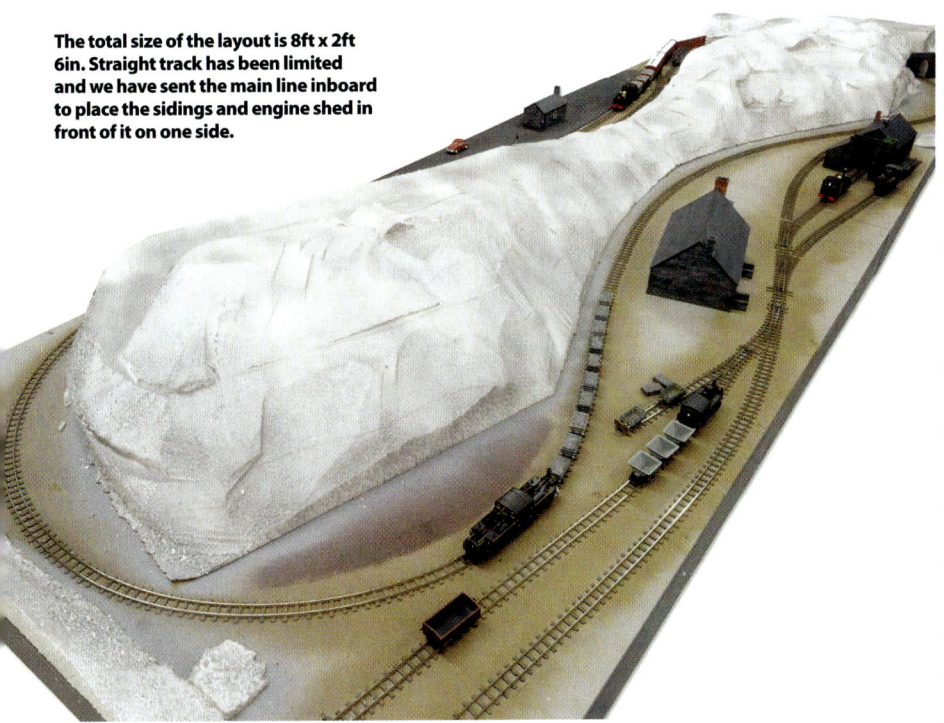

The total size of the layout is 8ft x 2ft 6in. Straight track has been limited and we have sent the main line inboard to place the sidings and engine shed in front of it on one side.

The scenic work may be at a very early stage, but it already has a whiff of Ffestiniog about the station scene. We can't wait to bring this to life.

Construction of the baseboards took around an hour and was followed promptly by assembly of three sets of legs – two to go underneath the first board with the third set positioned under the second board. The second board 'piggybacks' off the first and is bolted to it with M6 coach bolts. For added reliability and consistent alignment of the two boards during assembly, DCC Concepts alignment dowels were fitted to the joining faces of the baseboards.

The final step before track laying was painting of the baseboard surface and frame in a neutral grey colour to seal the wood and provide a base colour under the track when we laid it.

Track work

All of the track used on the layout is from the Peco 'OO9' range. In total, 10 yards of flexible track and eight points have been used in the trackplan which makes full use of the 8ft x 2ft 6in footprint.

One of the most critical elements of the plan was smooth curves, particularly as I was close to the minimum 2ft diameter radius with the trackplan for one end of the layout. To ensure a consistent curve of the same radius throughout I made a simple device for marking their position in pencil from an offcut of planed timber.

A centre point was marked at one end of the timber length to allow a single screw to pass through it into the baseboard. From this point measurements were set at 12in, 13in and 14in from the screw and 7mm holes were drilled through to allow a pencil to pass through the timber to draw lines on the baseboard surface. The idea worked a treat and gave me a centre line to work to on the 14in and 12in curves to be laid at each end of the circuit.

In this build I've aimed to avoid straight track as much as possible in the plan by gently curving all aspects of the line through the station and also by setting the sidings and engine shed in front of the main running line on the second side.

The track has all been pinned in place prior to the addition of dropper wires to take electricity from the main feed on each board to all the areas of the track. It has been wired for digital operation so all sidings are permanently live at all times which suits DCC and sound running. Once the wiring was complete, the entire layout was tested to ensure it worked as planned and happily I can report that it all worked first time leaving the way clear to move on to the scenic aspects.

A clean slate?

Right now the project is in the early stages of scenic development and you can expect a full feature on the scenic elements of the 'Fairlie Ambitious' layout in next issue's Staff Projects section. Plus you can also watch the build unfold in our latest KeyModelWorld TV show which is available to watch now on our website at www.keymodelworld.com/hornby-magazine-videos.

What I can say here and now is that the entire layout will have a slate theme to it. The buildings selected are all from Bachmann's narrow gauge range and include a slate engine shed, water tower, store, boiler room and chimney, bridge, tunnel mouth and a

WHAT WE USED		
PRODUCT	MANUFACTURER	CAT NO.
Main line left-hand point, 'OO9'	Peco	SL-E496
Main line right-hand point, 'OO9'	Peco	SL-E495
Right-hand point, 'OO9'	Peco	SL-E491
'Y' point, 'OO9'	Peco	SL-E497
Code 80 'OO9' narrow gauge plain track	Peco	SL-400
Code 80 rail joiners	Peco	SL-310
Code 80 insulated rail joiners	Peco	SL-311
Narrow gauge buffer stops	Peco	SL-440
Engine shed	Bachmann Scenecraft	44-0101
Water tower	Bachmann Scenecraft	44-0102
Coal store	Bachmann Scenecraft	44-0103
Hoist	Bachmann Scenecraft	44-0104
Slate Worker's cottage	Bachmann Scenecraft	44-0108
Slate processing building	Bachmann Scenecraft	44-0105
Slate boiler house and chimney	Bachmann Scenecraft	44-0106
Tunnel mouth	Bachmann Scenecraft	44-293
Slate footbridge	Bachmann Scenecraft	44-0107
Dark Brown spray paint	Humbrol	AD6029

slate worker's cottage which I'm repurposing as a station building (see panel for the full list).

Dividing the layout into two scenes means there will be a central spine of scenery and tunnels, bridges or cuttings at each end to both hide the curves and separate the scenes which are being built which as I type are in bare polystryrene. The idea is that the station area will have a raw slate wall immediately behind the rear platform giving rise to the scenery which will then fall gradually down to the sidings on the other side.

One element of the scenery is also still being considered and that is the question as to whether the land should fall away in front of the railway in at least one location on the board – a standout feature of the Ffestiniog Railway.

So far this new layout build has come together quite quickly. It's had about a day and a half put into it so far to make it into a working railway with a raw landscape ready for shaping. The next steps are all small ones which have to work around successive layers drying before the next can be applied, but it won't be long before this new narrow gauge layout is really taking shape and, hopefully, carrying off some of that wonderful character of the Ffestiniog Railway. Join me next month to see the finished layout and its scenic journey. ■

Earl of Merioneth stands outside the single road engine shed. A second track has been added in front of the shed to allow locomotives to take water.

The slate cottage from Bachmann Scenecraft is being repurposed as the station building. Positioned this way round you can't see that there isn't a door on the other side (although clearly this isn't a secret now!).

How it all starts: Bachmann's Scenecraft slate buildings collection, Peco 'OO9' track, Woodland Scenics products, 9mm plywood for the baseboard tops and planed timber for the frame and legs.

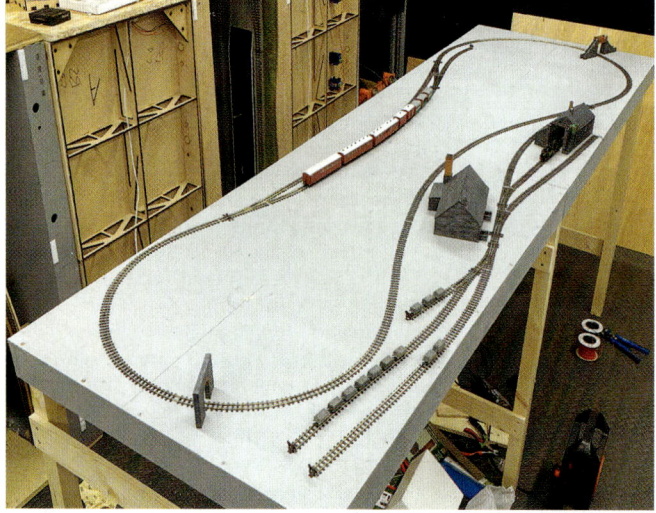

Not long after the start of track laying the full circuit and all of its sidings are complete. The track plan is relatively simple and incorporates 10 yards of track and eight points.

Polystyrene blocks were cut to shape then glued to the baseboard with PVA glue to create the raw landform. It will be shaped to suit using a hot wire foam cutter.

A trio of Fairlies meet at the the shed with Earl of Merioneth raising steam as Livingston Thompson eases slate wagons out of the yard and David Lloyd George passes on the main line with a passenger working.

Fairlie Good Idea – Part Two

Scenic modelling is one of the most enjoyable and creative parts of a model railway. **MIKE WILD** gets to grips with the landscape for the new 'OO9' narrow gauge layout in our second and final feature.

Building a model railway presents challenges and one of our greatest hurdles with this narrow gauge layout has been temperature and the cold snap at the beginning of December played havoc with drying times for our scenic project. On the positive side, that was our only challenge this time as we worked through a collection of established and new scenic products for the build.

We started building this new narrow gauge layout last issue (HM175). Its concept was inspired by the arrival of Bachmann's new 'OO9' narrow gauge Double Fairlie 0-4-4-0T, and we are certain that we won't be alone in seeing this model as a catalyst for a new layout. The idea, on paper, was simple: a quick project built over two or three days to fill a pair of 4ft x 2ft 6in baseboards which would generate a new backdrop for Hornby Magazine and KeyModelWorld narrow gauge features and become part of our permanent collection of model railways.

Cold snap aside, it's gone smoothly on the whole, though through the addition of more detail and features it has taken a little longer than we had originally planned. Last issue we showed it as a bare polystyrene landscape, but in this feature we have a largely completed (though I would hasten to add not finished) model railway with scenery around the full running line, working platform lamps, point motors, working ground signals and scenery which is representative of the open Welsh hills and impression of a slate covered mountain.

Multi-layers

All of our scenic work revolves around a layered approach. Each successive layer blends with the previous one and by the time we reach the end of the process any of the rough edges that might appear to be a problem at the start of scenery melt away under layers of grass, slate, powder and colours.

Having carved the landscape to shape, our first task was to add a double layer of plaster bandage over the scene to provide a hardshell onto which the scenic textures can be applied. This simple but messy job needs a little care and attention to ensure that track is protected from any accidental drips of plaster during application so we covered sections of the layout with scrap card. The plaster bandage was cut into 6in long strips to make them more manageable and laid over the bare polystyrene.

Immediately on completion, we painted the landscape using Burnt Umber acrylic from the Daler Rowney collection. We find painting the bare landscape at this stage allows some of the paint to sink into the plaster which limits the potential of white chips appearing should we accidentally knock the scenery.

The track is our next area of attention and having previously toned down the sleepers and rail sides with Humbrol No. 29 from a spray can, we added a little extra depth to the sleeper colours with some very brisk dry brushing of black and brown paints over the sleeper faces. Nothing too intense - just a little application to add a little colour and a job which took no more than five minutes to complete around the full layout.

From here it was into ground cover, starting with the ballast. For this narrow gauge layout we turned to our traditional choice of Woodland Scenics fine and medium grade Blended Gray ballast, but as it is a narrow gauge layout, our ratio of fine ballast was higher than it would be for a main line standard gauge line. We are never exact with our measurements for this as we prefer a little variation through the process, but a 50:50 or 60:40 ratio of medium to fine covers what we did here.

In most of our layout builds we have used diluted PVA glue to secure the ballast in position, but in recent projects we have

SKILLS GUIDE: LAYOUT CONSTRUCTION

switched to using SBR (Styrene Butadiene Rubber). This is a much thinner flexible adhesive which is used in building work and while it can be thinned with water during application it is water resistant when dry - unlike PVA. Its properties appear ideal for model railway ballasting and by wetting loose ballast with a water mister first we have found that SBR flows readily into the ballast and doesn't move ballast while it does so.

With the ballast complete and left to dry for at least 24 hours, the next phase was the start of general ground cover using Woodland Scenics fine blended green turf – a brilliant catch-all base colour for green scenery. This was added to the layout anywhere we would want to add static grasses in the future as well as around the edge of the goods yard at the slate sidings for a little extra depth - all held in place with PVA glue spread with a damp paint brush.

Potholed yard

A product we have been looking for the perfect place to use is Geoscenics Pot Holed Road kit. This does exactly what it says on the box by allowing a highly realistic rough road surface to be reproduced using the coloured powders included in the box.

To start, a layer of neat PVA was spread in the areas where the Pot Holed Road kit would be used which was then covered with the powder. As the powder went in, areas would build up depth and others would be lower and by adding more powder the surface can be built up including to create the ramps and infills for a road crossing over the railway lines on the approach to the shed. Once happy with the built up powder, we sprayed it with a mist of water then added PVA diluted in a 50:50 ratio with water to secure it in place.

While the yard surface was drying we set about casting rocks for the station side of the layout using Woodland Scenics Hydrocal and its series of rock moulds. With a large batch of castings to hand, they were added to the layout and then joined together with more Hydrocal with PVA added to the bare landscape and the back of each casing to aid adhesion.

These were one of the trickiest parts of the build as the cold outdoor temperatures really set in during the week that we were casting the rocks and affected drying times. Nevertheless, perseverance and patience paid off and having set some of the rocks without moulds, we set about carving the remainder to shape with a collection of chisels to create the final face.

Painting of the rocks was carried out in three phases. First came two coats of Natural Slate emulsion as a base colour which was then followed with a wash of thinned black acrylic to highlight the texture and detail in the rocks. We might be able to add more depth to the colour of the rocks in the future, but for now we are happy with how they are.

Slate mountain

An important feature of the narrow gauge layout was slate. Having coloured the rock castings in a suitable grey colour, attention turned to how we could include a hillside covered with tumbling slate, just like you might see from a train on the Ffestiniog Railway in North Wales.

At Fairlie Syniad Da station Livingston Thompson is ready to depart with a rake of slate wagons. Station lighting is with DCC Concepts station lamps which are now available through Gaugemaster.

Bachmann's narrow gauge slate buildings set the theme for the layout as Earl of Merioneth arrives in the yard with a rake of slate wagons.

WHAT WE USED		
PRODUCT	MANUFACTURER	CAT NO.
Burnt Umber acrylic paint	www.daler-rowney.com	223
Woodland Scenics fine blended gray ballast	www.bachmann.co.uk	B1393
Woodland Scenics medium blended gray ballast	www.bachmann.co.uk	B1394
Woodland Scenics fine blended green turf	www.bachmann.co.uk	T1349
Pot Holed Road kit	www.geoscenics.co.uk	PH600
Woodland Scenics Hydrocal	www.bachmann.co.uk	C1201
Woodland Scenics rock moulds	www.bachmann.co.uk	Various
Woodland Scenics 7mm medium green static grass	www.bachmann.co.uk	FS622
Woodland Scenics light green coarse turf	www.bachmann.co.uk	T1363
Woodland Scenics burnt grass coarse turf	www.bachmann.co.uk	T1362
Medium spring static grass	www.green-scenes.co.uk	n/a
Medium summer static grass	www.green-scenes.co.uk	n/a
Long spring static grass	www.green-scenes.co.uk	n/a
Long summer static grass	www.green-scenes.co.uk	n/a
Fine dark stone	www.wwscenics.co.uk	07-1019-VAR014
Coarse dark stone	www.wwscenics.co.uk	11-0918-VAR018
Custom 3D printed station nameboards	www.cheekytek.com	n/a

3D printed accessories from Modelu, fire irons and weathering all add to the scene around the single road engine shed.

War World Scenics was our port of call as it produces a range of crushed slate coloured rocks in different grades. By using its coarse and fine dark stone products, we were able to replicate a slate covered hillside which was secured in place with a combination of a base layer of neat PVA and followed by diluted PVA added over the top to hold all the slate together.

From here the ground cover focus was on static grasses. The first layer was applied over a 60:40 mix of PVA and water and left to dry before the addition of a final flurry of ground cover textures including more static grasses and fine and coarse turfs. These final layers were held in place with matt varnish from an aerosol which allows multiple layers to be built up on top of one another immediately to create detailed and dense ground cover. When doing this, we use a piece of scrap cardboard as a mask to prevent unwanted spray going on the track – this is particularly important with static grasses as they will stick anywhere where there is adhesive!

The finishing touches for the ground cover were pieces of Woodland Scenics fine leaf foliage around the top edge of the rock faces behind the station as well as selected pieces around the scene to hide scenic joints and blend elements together.

One thing you might notice is the lack of trees on the raised central spine of scenery, which is quite deliberate. We wanted the landscape to appear windswept and open, rather than being overpopulated with vegetation. In addition, there was also the possibility of overcomplicating the height of the layout and dominating the buildings with trees.

Final detailing

With a landscape complete, attention turned to adding the final details. At the station, DCC Concepts working ground signals connected via the new Ground Signal Interface control boards to Cobalt point motors were added. These switch aspect with the changing of the point to indicate a green or red aspect depending on whether the line ahead is clear or not. These were brilliantly simple to install, taking around five minutes per junction through their plug and play wiring system.

Next the electrical additions continued with platform lamps added using an old set of DCC Concepts gas lamps (now available through Gaugemaster) which were wired through to their own 12V DC power supply. This has also been used to power lights in the station building, engine shed and slate processing structure.

The platform surface has been dressed with a light coat of Geoscenics Pot Holed Road kit grey powder and then furnished with benches from Dart Castings, a handful of figures, luggage trollies and custom 3D printed station signs from CheekyTek. There are also figures from Modelu3D, Scenecraft and Noch.

Moving around to the shed and yard, these are the areas where we can go to town the most. The shed roads have been weathered further with MIG rail weathering paints while details including standpipes, oil supply cans and hoses from Modelu3D plus barrels, spare shovels and other accessories from our spares box.

The slate yard benefits from the addition of piled slate, vehicles, figures and sacks of prepared slate waiting for onward movement by rail, although we feel there is more that we can add to this area in the future.

Fairlie Syniad Da

Building a narrow gauge continuous run layout has been an exciting and involving project. Its compact nature means that this two-board layout will be quick to dismantle and assemble while its features make it an attractive scene to watch the trains go by or operate. With DCC control, the yard can be shunted independently of the main line while the engine shed can be treated in the same way creating an engaging railway despite its relatively small size.

The arrival of Bachmann's Double Fairlie was the inspiration for this layout and it has brought new ideas with it too. The completed layout, we hope, will remind you of trips on narrow gauge railways in North Wales where coach footboards skim the grass, tiny slate wagons rattle along behind attractive engines and the scenery dominates the view.

And if you were wondering about the station name, its Welsh for 'Fairlie Good Idea'. ∎

David Lloyd George enters Fairlie Syniad Da with a passenger set headed by a trio of Ffestiniog Railway 'Bug Box' coaches.

The narrow tunnel through the scenery is typical of a narrow gauge line. Livingston Thompson is in charge of the slate train.

Limited editions | Exclusive products | Modelling essentials | Limited editions

KEY Publishing Model World MODELLING SHOP

NEW LIMITED EDITIONS

NEW! HORNBY CROSSCOUNTRY HST LIMITED EDITION power cars 43184 & 43366 in 'OO' Gauge.

DCC Ready **£359.99**
DCC Sound Fitted **£399.99**

PRE-ORDER

CAVALEX MODELS Class 60 60029 for 'OO' Gauge

DCC Ready **£194.95**
DCC Sound Fitted **SOLD OUT**

PRE-ORDER

BACHMANN 40145 for 'OO' Gauge

DCC Ready **£229.95**
DCC Sound Fitted **£329.95**

IN STOCK NOW

EXCLUSIVE BUNDLE Hornby Rail Charter Services HST power cars, coaches and book

Price **£499.99**

IN STOCK NOW

HELJAN Class 47/8 47817 for 'OO' Gauge

DCC Ready **£249.95**
DCC Sound Fitted **£389.95**

PRE-ORDER

ACCURASCALE Class 31 31276 for 'OO' Gauge

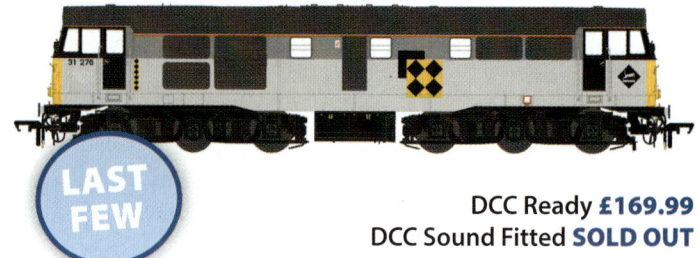

LAST FEW

DCC Ready **£169.99**
DCC Sound Fitted **SOLD OUT**

EXCLUSIVE PRODUCTS AND MODELLING ESSENTIALS

GSMR Radio Masts Twin Pack for OO gauge
£5.99

LBSCR Sydenham Station Building Laser-Cut Kit for OO gauge
£75.99

GNR Laser-Cut Signalbox Kit for OO gauge
£32.99

BR Diesel Brake Tender B964040E Plain BR Green
£36.99

TT:120 Scale Laser-Cut Platform Kit - Option B
£32.99

TT:120 Scale Laser-Cut Platform Kit - Option A
£37.99

OO Gauge Laser-Cut GNR Tunnel Portal Kit
£54.99

TT:120 Scale Laser-Cut GNR Tunnel Portal Kit
£29.99

OO Gauge Laser-Cut Viaduct Outer Twin Arch Kit
£119.99

OO Gauge Laser-Cut Viaduct Single Inner Arch Kit
£119.99
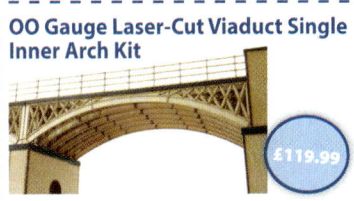

3D printed Larssen steel piling triple pack 50mm high
£14.99

3D printed Larssen steel piling triple pack 100mm high
£22.99

3D Printed OO Gauge Axle Counters - 10 Pack
£2.99

Single-bay low relief warehouse entrance kit
£12.99

Four-bay low relief warehouse laser-cut kit
£44.99
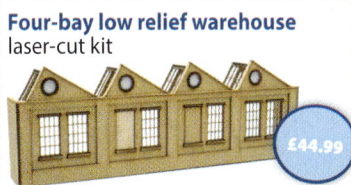

WCML Relay Room 00 Gauge Laser Cut Kit
£34.99

Norton Bridge Signalbox 00 Gauge Laser Cut Kit
£47.99

Norton Bridge 3D printed signalbox interior kit
£12.99
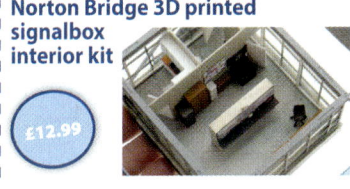

GCR Birdcage Bridge and walls laser-cut kit for OO Gauge
£79.99

GCR Birdcage Bridge laser-cut kit for OO Gauge
£64.99

PJM Models laser-cut four-road diesel depot and office kit - B
£135.00
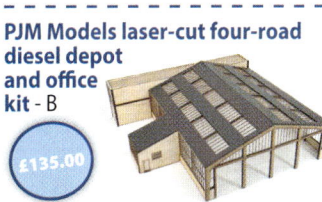

PJM Models laser-cut four-road diesel depot kit - A
£85.00
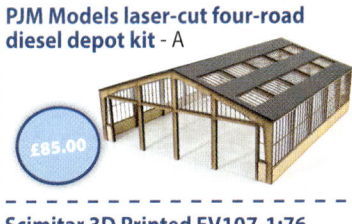

Pot Hole Road Kit
£13.49
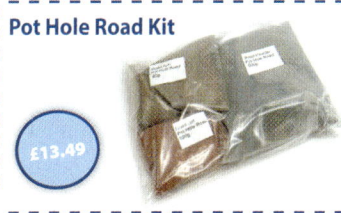

Airbrush Starter Bundle
£460.00

Scorpion 3D Printed FV101-1:76 OO Scale Tank Kit
£11.99

Scimitar 3D Printed FV107-1:76 OO Scale Tank Kit
£11.99

Scorpion 3D Printed FV107-1:43 O Scale Tank Kit
£34.99

Scimitar 3D Printed FV107-1:43 O Scale Tank Kit
£34.99

RUSTY RAILS MODELLING 3D PRINTED ACCESSORIES

View the full range of Rusty Rails 'OO' gauge 3D printed depot and lineside products on the Key Model World Shop.

Visit: shop.keymodelworld.com/collections/rusty-rails-modelling

IN STOCK NOW

Scan the QR code for full details of all our modelling products on our online shop:

keymodelworld.com/shop

SKILLS GUIDE: LAYOUT CONSTRUCTION

Track laying

A fundamental component of a model railway is track. **NIGEL BURKIN** presents his guide to successful tracklaying for newcomers to railway modelling.

MOST NEWCOMERS to our hobby quickly become acquainted with sectional track systems, especially if they've started with a trainset. Trainsets usually include a basic oval of track and perhaps a siding or two. They can be expanded with track packs and additional pieces to increase the system within a neatly defined geometry.

Sectional track is ideally designed for setting out temporary layouts on a tabletop or the floor for a rainy Sunday afternoon of operations and then put away in its boxes once the session is over. Such layouts can be made permanent too when laid out on a baseboard and the track may be coloured and ballasted for a more realistic appearance.

Many experienced modellers are familiar with track sections such as Hornby R600 and R601; the geometry of the sectional track curves and how it all fits together with adequate clearances on curves. This is a neat and convenient way to build up a layout without having to think about clearances and cutting flexible track, and many experienced modellers probably cut their modelling teeth on Hornby or Peco track systems.

From Peco to Atlas, the more advanced flexible track systems are supplemented with sectional track pieces. Furthermore, there are track systems with moulded ballast bases which are perfect for building up temporary layouts including the 'N' and 'OO' gauge Unitrack system by Kato.

Flexibility
Flexible track systems are a step up from set track and offer the modeller more freedom to

When assembling set track, be sure to check all rail joiners to see that they are correctly aligned and there are no kinks in the track.

Above: Misaligned rail joiners are guaranteed to derail some if not all of the trains run on a set track layout.

Left: Tools for tracklaying including pin vice, track templates, modelling knife and a means of cutting flexible track to length, including cutting discs and the popular Xuron track cutters.

THE STAGES OF TRACKLAYING

- Complete the baseboard tops
- Mark in the proposed track formation using photocopies of the turnouts as templates and lengths of plain track to set out the formations
- Fit the track underlay – it may be composed of cork, foam or a moulded material
- Work out the position of under track devices, if any, and prepare the trackbed to accept them
- Lay the track using gauges and clearance tools
- Wire up the track for power - fit operating devices such as point motors and test everything extensively
- Paint the track, rails and surrounding area of baseboard
- Ballasting, rail cleaning and weathering

create bespoke track formations. Manufacturers usually offer matching turnouts made with greater diverging angles to go with flexible track products. Smoother flowing track and junctions together with increased realism is possible, at the cost of losing the temporary nature of the layout.

Flexible track allows the modeller to shape curves into the track to create a wide range of layout designs, limited by the minimum radius curves that the rolling stock can reliably negotiate. Whilst flexible track may be stiff enough to hold any shape introduced to it, flexible track cannot really be used to make temporary tabletop layouts.

With flexible track comes more serious layout building with track firmly fixed in place, »

Well laid track is essential to the successful operation of a model railway. At Grosvenor Square, *Hornby Magazine's* Western Region terminus, features a complex junction formation, all of which is laid with Peco Code 75 track.

SKILLS GUIDE: LAYOUT CONSTRUCTION

Sectional track is easy for newcomers to use and with the right care and attention it can look very good in appearance. A small test section was built for this article using some Hornby track pieces.

Model railway track comes in many forms, from set track pieces and extension packs to flexible track systems and components for kit and hand-built track. No matter which type you prefer to use, the basic principles of tracklaying remain the same.

Permanently laying track on a baseboard is preferable to creating temporary layouts on carpet or wooden floors where dirt, fluff and hairs can be a problem. To improve performance, consider using dense foam or cork track underlay.

either using glue or track pins and with the potential for considerably more scenic treatment. Popular systems include Peco Streamline for 'OO' and 'N' gauge which is compatible with all British ready-to-run rolling stock. Peco has recently introduced bullhead rail flexible track and points which have scale sleeper spacings too. Other flexible track systems include Tillig which is gaining in popularity in the UK. Flexible track is offered by companies regarded as 'finescale' including C&L Finescale and Marcway for use with turnout kits and individual track components.

There is nothing to prevent you from mixing and matching track systems to suit your layout plans, so long as they have the same rail profile or adapter sections are used. The most common rail profile is Code 100, used in all British set track systems, while finescale rail profiles such as Code 75 are available only as flexible track and larger radii points. Given the use of Code 100 profile track, set track can be used with flexible track to make a formation fit a given space. »

The first step is to lay track underlay (cork in this case) which has been cut to width and is being glued in place using a waterproof PVA glue.

Inspect the rail joiners for misalignment and run a finger over them to find any rough spots that could prevent trains from running smoothly over the layout.

Left: A pin vice and twist drill are used to drill through the sleepers and part way into the baseboard top, to a depth of approximately ⅔ of the length of the track pins. Track pins may be pushed into the holes without bending them or distorting the track. Note the centreline for track alignment (A); pin hole moulded in the Hornby set track (B) and pin vice used to drill into the baseboard top (C) to ease the use of track pins.

10 top tips
FOR LAYING TRACK

During tracklaying and also when planning the layout, test clearances with the longest vehicles to be operated on the layout to determine your minimum clearance measurement. The sharper the curves, particularly when using set track, the greater the chance of stock touching when passing on double track sections.

A gentle rub with fine grade wet and dry paper soon removes any rough edges or burrs.

1. Before diving straight in, plan your track carefully, ensuring you have the right materials and look at ways in which the track for large layouts can be laid in phases to spread the cost and make the task of wiring and testing easier to do. To work out if your trackplan will fit your space, take turnouts to a copy shop and photocopy them. Check levels carefully and take note of any possible inclines – are they likely to be too steep for your trains?

2. Track on the full size railway is laid on specially prepared ground which has been levelled and graded for the smoothest transition into curves and gradients and covered by a layer of ballast. Ballast holds the track in place and provides the all-important drainage to keep the water flowing away from the line. To make your track look more realistic, do not lay it flat on the baseboard top - use either cork or dense underlay foam to raise it above the baseboard level.

3. Track pins are a favourite way of securing track to the layout and are easily removed when adjustments to the track are required, at least until it is ballasted. When using sectional track, use the holes provided for track pins. Flexible track systems rarely have pinholes, leaving it to you to drill your own using a pin vice. Use a drill slightly thicker than your pins, drill clean through the sleepers and into the baseboard top to about ⅔ of the length of the pins. Apply pins using pliers or a light hammer.

4. Should you find the sight of track pins unsightly, consider removing them after ballasting the track. Dilute PVA or cements formulated for scenery work are strong enough to hold track in place, making the track pins, at least the majority of them, unnecessary. There are alternative techniques for securing track including white glue and double sided foam tape.

5. There are numerous techniques for cutting track into desired lengths. Track cutters have become a popular tool for quick trimming of rails to speed up tracklaying. Rails can be cut using a cutting disc fitted to a minidrill. It is a less precise cutting method because the disc can slip on the rail.

6. When cutting flexible track to length, save any surplus sleepers that may become detached. They are used to fill in gaps between track sections where they are joined with rail joiners. To accommodate rail joiners, the web under the rails together with the rail clips at the end of the track length must be trimmed.

7. Consideration has to be given to the location of uncoupling devices, particularly those fitted under the track. When the track formation has been decided upon the position of any under track device should be determined and a hole of the appropriate size cut in both track bed and baseboard top before track is laid.

8. Remember that your stock has a say in your plans too - the sharper the curves you plan to use, the greater the overhang with bogie stock. Some stock may not be able to negotiate sharp curves and it is worth doing some tests to see if your planned minimum radius curve is acceptable to the locomotives and stock you wish to run.

9. Allow for heat expansion and contraction when laying track. Rails on a model railway expand in much the same manner as those of the full size railway. Avoid laying track in particularly cold or hot conditions so expansion gaps are not exaggerated when temperatures drop or become closed too soon after temperatures rise.

10. Tracklaying is only a part of the story. Once track is in place, it has to be equipped with turnout motors and wired up (assuming you want to use point motors, of course). Do not start any scenic work or ballasting until it has been wired up and extensively tested with all of your stock. Look for faults such as misaligned rail joiners you have missed.

SKILLS GUIDE: LAYOUT CONSTRUCTION

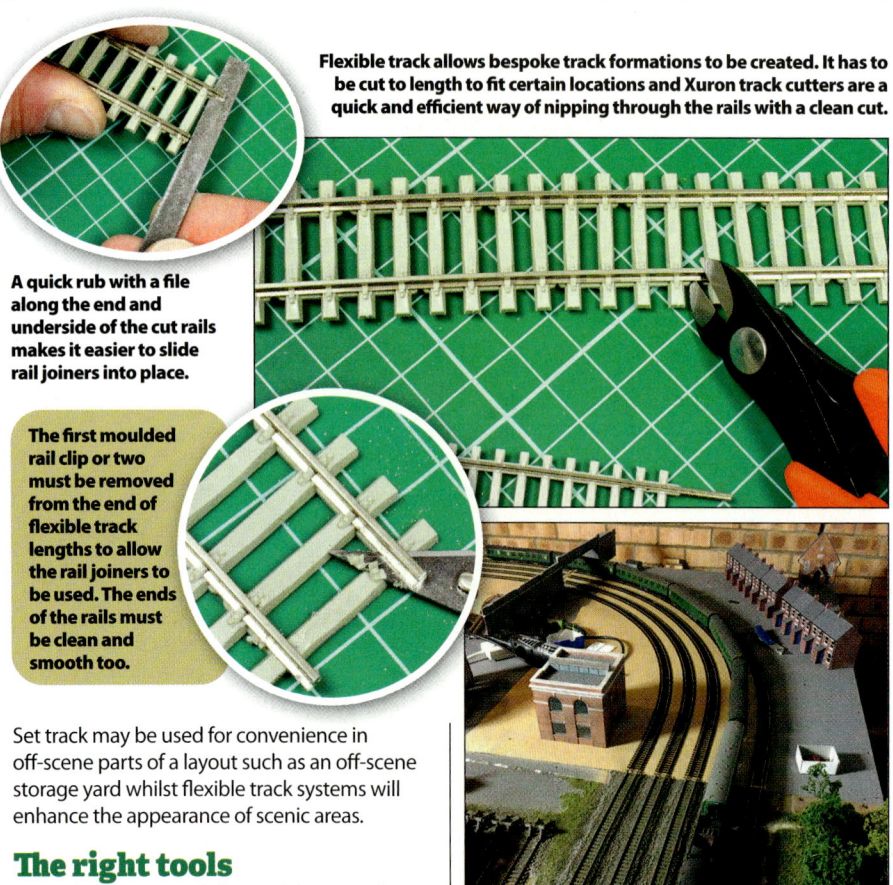

A quick rub with a file along the end and underside of the cut rails makes it easier to slide rail joiners into place.

Flexible track allows bespoke track formations to be created. It has to be cut to length to fit certain locations and Xuron track cutters are a quick and efficient way of nipping through the rails with a clean cut.

The first moulded rail clip or two must be removed from the end of flexible track lengths to allow the rail joiners to be used. The ends of the rails must be clean and smooth too.

Set track may be used for convenience in off-scene parts of a layout such as an off-scene storage yard whilst flexible track systems will enhance the appearance of scenic areas.

The right tools

Using the correct tools for track laying will make the task easier, quicker and will produce a better result. Whilst there is no need to buy specialist tools, there are certain ones which will be needed no matter which type of system you use. When laying set track on a baseboard, you will need a small hammer to apply track pins, a pin vice for holding twist drills and a pair of fine nose pliers for handling rail joiners.

When using flexible track, the aforementioned small hammer, pin vice, drills and pliers are all necessary. You will also need some way of cutting flexible track to length to fit track formations. Some modellers like to use a cutting disc and minidrill (use eye protection). Others like to use specialised track cutting shears from Xuron and DCC Concepts. Files are needed to clean away any burrs from the cut end of the rail whichever method you use.

Consumable materials include track pins, adhesives, rail joiners, track underlay and some shims of 10 thou styrene for levelling. Gauges such as Tracksetta are very helpful for achieving straight track lengths or curves of a given radius using flexible track.

Flexible track allows smooth flowing curves of any radius to be laid. Here the extension to *Hornby Magazine's* Twelve Trees Junction is shown in the early stages of track laying with the new curves taking the line back to the storage yard. All of this is laid with Peco code 75 flexible track.

Finally, give thought to the type of point or turnout motor you plan to use and buy in enough to complete each phase of tracklaying. Preparation of the trackbed to accommodate point motors may need to be completed before track and points are fixed to the layout – see pages 70-73. The same applies to many proprietary under-the-track uncoupling magnets and, in both cases, read the instructions to see what is required before placing track underlay and the track itself.

Give some thought as to how track on the full size railway appears and how you can make your layout track look as good in model form, even when you plan to use set track pieces. Colour has an important part to play together with choosing the right ballast, both in size and colour. Spend some time studying photographs of track and make notes on colour, texture, the type of track and how it becomes weathered through long term use and exposure to the elements. Then the fun of making scenery can commence! ■

When glued in place, the gaps in the foam resulting from the cuts are not too wide and the track will be fully supported. Ballasting will hide any evidence of your underlay tricks!

Flexible track is linked with plastic webs between the sleepers. They make the assembly of track sections easier during manufacturing. However, some flexible track is stiff. When laying curved sections consider cutting into the web between the sleepers to free it up should it be required.

Right: Cork and foam underlay can be laid to curves too. This picture shows how to slice part way through the width of underlay foam so it may be laid to a tight curve. The cuts are made on the outside edge of the curve.

Left: Tracksetta is an extremely useful range of gauging tools designed for use with flexible track in 'OO' and 'N' gauges. An 'N' gauge Tracksetta of 15in radius is shown. It has slots along its length to enable track pins to be used.

The materials and process of tracklaying is demonstrated with Hornby R600 straight set track pieces, Woodland Scenics ballast and painted weathering effects on this small diorama. Starting from bare baseboard at the bottom left of the picture: A) The track centreline drawn in place to assist with accurate alignment of the track. B) Cork has been used as trackbed to raise it above baseboard level. C) Baseboard tops must be strong and rigid enough to provide track with a flat surface. D) Hornby track before painting and weathering. E) Sleepers are painted before ballasting. F) Rail edges are painted with rust colours. G) The surrounding baseboard (the cess) is painted too. H) A ballast shoulder is created by piling ballast against the edge of the cork underlay. Grasses are applied up to the cess but not onto the ballast shoulder when modelling a main line.

Expansion should be catered for by leaving a small gap at each join in the track. A piece of 20 thou styrene is ideal as a gauge for making expansion gaps in 'N' gauge, with 30 or 40 thou preferred in 'OO' gauge.

Another view of tracklaying underway, this time with Atlas code 55 track. Fine nose pliers are useful for sliding rail joiners in place (A) and rail clips have been pared away from two sleepers (B) to allow rail joiners to be used without forcing them onto the rail ends. This track has been glued into place carefully to avoid too much glue from squeezing up between the sleepers (C) and making a mess.

Track types can be mixed on one layout. This junction formation uses a mix of kit-built turnouts and flexible track made by C&L Finescale, track components by Peco and handbuilt track using copper-clad sleeper strip. All the rail profiles are the same, even if the sleeper type is different.

USEFUL WEBSITES	
Hornby	www.hornby.com
Bachmann	www.bachmann.co.uk
Peco	www.peco-uk.com
Tillig	www.tillig.com

With practice the basics of track laying can be used to create a track layout as complex as your imagination and space allows and with flowing curves too.

SKILLS GUIDE: LAYOUT CONSTRUCTION

Point motors

Motorising points makes a model railway more realistic and easier to operate. **MIKE WILD** explains how solenoid point motors are installed and how to connect them for analogue and digital control.

MOTORISED POINTS are a great feature to add to a model railway and with the right tools, equipment and knowledge they can be simple and quick to install. In this guide we explain how to install Peco solenoid point motors – a readily available product which can be bought for a few pounds.

The majority of this guide is relevant to Gaugemaster's and Rails of Sheffield's solenoids too, all of which work on the same principles – the main differences being in how they mount to a layout.

Deciding on how you will operate point motors is just as important as their installation. The primary choices are analogue and digital and we have explained the basics of both in the step by step guide. Making bigger layouts with more points is simply a case of repeating the steps over and over to reach the end result – and thinking through your wiring plan.

There are alternatives on both fronts. For analogue, you have the choice of stud and probe, toggle and push button switches (all will require a 16v AC power supply and a Capacitor Discharge Unit (CDU) for reliable operation) while digital layout builders have a wide range of choice when it comes to accessory decoders.

We've used many brands on *Hornby Magazine's* layouts over the years, but by the far the strongest and most dependable decoders for solenoid point motors are DCC Concepts' ADS series which are available in two and eight output formats. For this guide we have used Train Tech's quadport accessory decoders – another well regarded choice in the *Hornby Magazine* office.

Also worthy of mention are stall motors such as DCC Concepts' Cobalt and the Tortoise. Both of these are regularly referred to as slow action motors and, rather than having solenoids which 'fire' the point blades, they have geared motors which move the point blades across in a realistic manner. They are more expensive, but are much more feature-rich with the Cobalt including built in frog switching, feedback and control options for digital and analogue.

One final product range to mention is DCC Concepts' Alpha Panel system. This impressive set of plug and play electronics allows a professional standard control panel to be developed at home using a selection of illuminated panel mounted switches and circuit boards which can be connected to any digital control system for point operation. ■

WHAT WE USED		
PRODUCT	**MANUFACTURER**	**CAT NO.**
Extended pin point motor	www.peco-uk.com	PL-10E
Point motor mounting base	www.peco-uk.com	PL-9
7 x 0.2mm multi-core equipment wire	www.rapidonline.com	GW010435
Quad-port accessory decoder	www.gaugemasterretail.com	TTPC200

STEP BY STEP: INSTALLING SOLENOID POINT MOTORS

Skill Level: Intermediate

TOOLS
» Craft knife
» Soldering iron
» Wire strippers
» Side cutters
» Flatblade screwdriver
» Crosshead screwdriver
» Pin vice and 1mm drill
» Pin hammer
» Electric drill
» 8mm drill bit

1 Point motor installation begins by preparing the baseboard to accommodate the actuating rod which will move the point blades from side to side. The first three steps relate to any type of below-baseboard installation. First, mark the maximum throw position of the blades using the central holes in a '00' gauge point. We do this with a 1mm drill bit in a pin vice.

2 Make pen marks at the outer ends of the tie bar to assist in locating the 1mm holes. An 8mm diameter hole can then be drilled through the baseboard to accommodate the throw of the point motor actuating rod.

3 Return the point to its original position taking care to ensure that the previously drilled hole is visible through the centre hole in the tie bar at both end of its movement.

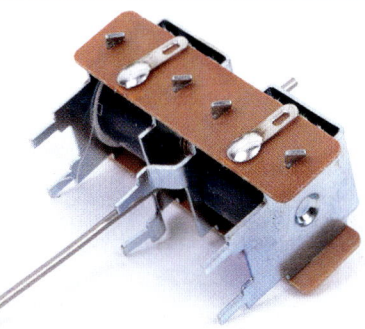

4 Now we need to prepare each motor for fitting. This is a repeated process for each motor that we find easiest to do in batches. This is the base ingredient – a Peco extended pin solenoid point motor which can be mounted beneath the baseboard completely out of sight.

Changing points with point motors makes for much more realistic operation and has equal benefits for home and portable layouts. At St Stephens Road a 'Warship' hydraulic stands in the platform road to wait for a Collett '2251' 0-6-0 to clear the single line.

ELECTRICS

SKILLS GUIDE: LAYOUT CONSTRUCTION

STEP BY STEP: INSTALLING SOLENOID POINT MOTORS

5  To prepare the motor for installation, we fitted a PL9 mounting plate to the motor. This simply slides over the tags on the top of the motor frame and the tags are then folded over to secure the two components together. Use a small flatblade screwdriver to bend the tags.

6 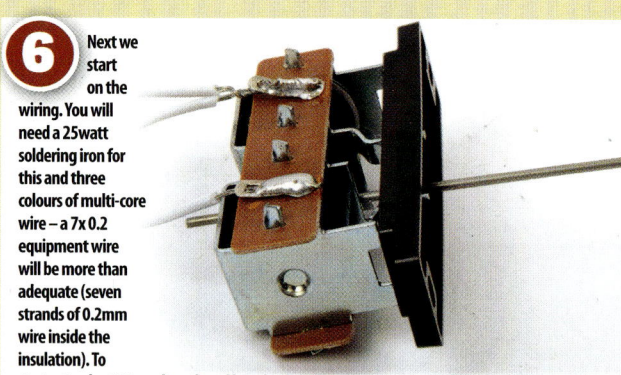 Next we start on the wiring. You will need a 25watt soldering iron for this and three colours of multi-core wire – a 7x 0.2 equipment wire will be more than adequate (seven strands of 0.2mm wire inside the insulation). To start cut a short 75mm length and bare both ends using wire strippers. Then, bare the end of another length – we used 3ft lengths for the main leads – and twist two ends together. These are connected to one terminal and the other bared end of the shorter wire to the other terminal. This is the common return side of the point motor.

7  Once you have soldered the white wire in place, turn the motor over and cut two 3ft lengths of red and green wire – these are the power feeds which actuate the solenoids to make the point motor move from side to side. Solder these onto the two tags and ensure that every further point motor you do has the same arrangement of coloured cables – that way they will all operate the same way round.

8 Repeat the process of fitting mounting plates and wires and you will end up with a collection of point motors looking like this. These are all now ready to install underneath a layout.

9  Using the pre-drilled 8mm holes in the baseboard, motors can be fitted in place underneath the point they operate. For convenience, all were fitted in the same orientation – green and red wires to the left, white to the right. When installing these motors they need to be adjusted carefully for perfect operation – the motor should move freely underneath and the point blades should also move freely when it is correctly fitted. No. 4 ½in screws were used to secure the baseplates to the baseboard, which also allow for a little adjustment if necessary.

10  When it comes to powering point motors there are two choices: digital or analogue. First we will show how to power them with digital control using a Train-Tech quad-port accessory decoder (now part of the Gaugemaster range). This process is the same for all types of point motor accessory decoder. Full instructions are supplied with them. First, fix the decoder block to the baseboard using No. 4 ½in screws.

11  Cut the wires of the first point motor to length allowing at least 2in of flexibility. Bare the ends with wire strippers then twist the multi-core strands together and fold them in half – this gives a strong connection for the terminals on the accessory decoder.

12  Insert the wires into the terminals. The white from our point motor is the common return so this always goes into the centre terminal of each output on the Train Tech decoder. We then fitted green to terminal 2 and red to terminal 1 as standard throughout this layout project.

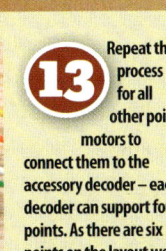

13 Repeat the process for all other point motors to connect them to the accessory decoder – each decoder can support four points. As there are six points on the layout we used two PC2 decoders and wired them logically so that the station run-round loop is operated by accessory outputs 1-4 and the goods yard by 5-6.

14 As a final step, the accessory decoder now needs connecting to the DCC power supply. We link the central pair of red and green wires directly back to the controller connection point on this layout for simplicity. For bigger layouts it may be necessary to provide a separate power feed through a booster to operate the point motors as solenoids have a high current draw. The accessory decoder can then be addressed as detailed in the instruction sheet using their one-touch learning button.

15 Having tested all the motors operate correctly under power, the final step is to remove the excess pin from the point motor protruding above the baseboard. Use either a pair of sharp side cutters or carefully cut the excess off with a cutting disc in a minidrill. Be aware though that the heat generated by this method can melt plastic, so cut partway through each one, allowing them to cool before continuing.

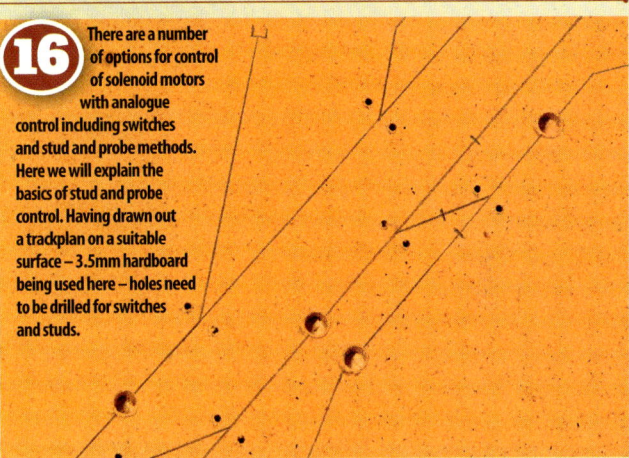

16 There are a number of options for control of solenoid motors with analogue control including switches and stud and probe methods. Here we will explain the basics of stud and probe control. Having drawn out a trackplan on a suitable surface – 3.5mm hardboard being used here – holes need to be drilled for switches and studs.

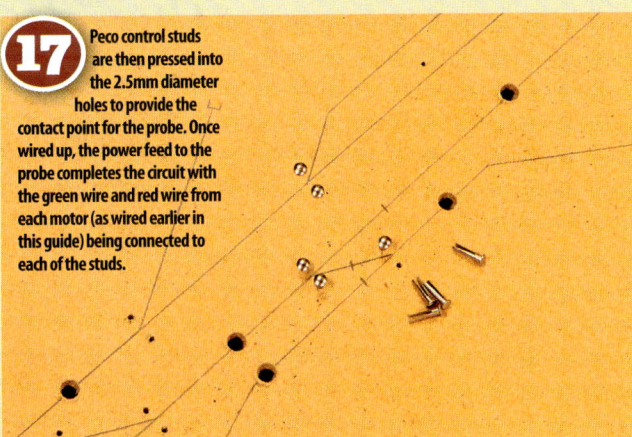

17 Peco control studs are then pressed into the 2.5mm diameter holes to provide the contact point for the probe. Once wired up, the power feed to the probe completes the circuit with the green wire and red wire from each motor (as wired earlier in this guide) being connected to each of the studs.

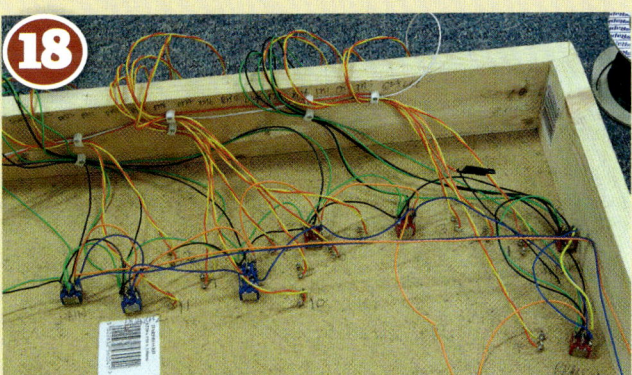

18 Looking underneath the panel, the red and yellow wires here are the control wires for the point motors which would join to the red and green wires on the motors shown earlier in this sequence.

19 The final component is a Capacitor Discharge Unit (CDU). This is essential for reliable operation of solenoid motors as it stores a charge of power which gives a positive throw to the point. The red and white wires going to the right go back to the 16v AC power supply while the red and white wires going to the left go to the probe (red) and common return (white) connection on the point motors.

20 A stud and probe control panel can be built to suit any layout of any shape or size. The probe completes the circuit and when it contacts the studs sends power to one side of the solenoid motor or the other to operate the coils, throwing the point blades for the route required.

SKILLS GUIDE: LAYOUT CONSTRUCTION

Ballasting

The railway uses ballast to hold the track in place and provide drainage, but in model form it is a cosmetic feature which can make or break a layout. **MARK CHIVERS** explains the principles and shows how you can achieve brilliant ballast in miniature.

BALLAST is an essential component of any railway large or small - and replicating it in model form is a straightforward task with the right materials, glues and a handy dose of patience.

The first thing to understand is how ballast is used on the real railway. It is there to hold the track in place and provide drainage, but different areas of the railway call for a variety of ballast styles. Main lines require a shoulder used to support the edges of the track while in a station environment that feature won't be so pronounced. In depots and yards, it will be virtually non-existent while in a locomotive depot ballast will be a rare commodity. Instead (for steam era depots at least) you will find ash and cinders crushed between the sleepers holding the track in place.

Another consideration for accurate ballast is the location and its age. For example, ballast in the Scottish Highlands has a pink hue while most other areas have varying grades of grey depending on age. Materials weather with time with the centre of the running lines

A Hughes-Fowler 'Crab' 2-6-0 leads a mixed goods through the bridge onto the newly ballasted section of main line. Weathering is at an early stage here with the first applications of Geoscenics Track Grime and Black done. More will be added later once these first layers have fully dried.

gaining the most staining, while at stations, and anywhere where locomotives stand, black staining will appear too.

Having observed the real railway for inspiration, we can start developing our model ballast. This feature really can make or break a layout's scenery – and when done right it complements the rolling stock which runs on the track beautifully.

There are several options. Foam covered with ballast granules is available for sectional track pieces and there are also ballast mats which can be laid underneath the track. None of these compare to the potential of loose ballasting a model railway by hand. It's a time-honoured process which most exhibition layouts and thousands of home layouts use. The most important ingredient in getting it right is time and patience. Ballasting is not a job to be rushed.

Loose ballast is available from many manufacturers including Woodland Scenics, DCC Concepts, Gaugemaster, Peco, Natural Scenics, Javis, Hornby, Green Scene and more. Top of the charts in the *Hornby Magazine* office are Woodland Scenics and DCC Concepts products. For this guide, we will use Woodland Scenics blended grey ballast in fine and medium grades to match the previous ballasting on earlier parts of this scenic layout.

What you will need to hand are a plastic tub, two grades of ballast, a paint brush and adhesive. For this guide, we use Deluxe Materials Ballast Bond, but a 50:50 mixture of PVA wood glue with water and a drop of detergent applied with a syringe will reap the same result should you choose to. This was our first time using Deluxe Materials' Ballast Bond and we were wholly impressed at its ability to flow into the ballast without the need for pre-wetting with a water mister.

The step by step guide explains the process from start to finish. ■

WHAT WE USED		
PRODUCT	MANUFACTURER	CAT NO.
Blended grey medium grade ballast	Woodland Scenics	B1393
Blended grey fine grade ballast	Woodland Scenics	B1394
Ballast Bond	Deluxe Materials	AD75
Roket fine tips (six pack)	Deluxe Materials	AC20
Track Grime paint	Geoscenics	TG50
Black Concentrate paint	Geoscenics	BC50

TOOLS
» Plastic tub
» ½in or 1in paintbrush
» Patience!

SKILLS GUIDE: LAYOUT CONSTRUCTION

STEP BY STEP: BALLASTING A MODEL RAILWAY

1 The first steps are in preparing this main line scene for ballast. We've recently laid the track over a 1/16in cork sheet, but it now needs trimming back around the running lines to create the ballast shoulder we want.

2 Using a craft knife with a fresh blade, cut through the cork along the edge of each side of the track.

3 Now simply pick up one end of the cut strip and pull. This will remove the central strip of cork sheet allowing the track to stand proud of the baseboard surface.

4 Continuing the same process, the cork around all four of our main line tracks has now been trimmed back. The final step is to clear away the tools and any debris from track laying.

5 Basic weathering of the track comes next. In this case we needed to cover previously completed ballast and buildings using a combination of masking tape and scrap A4 sheets of paper. Take your time and ensure that anything you don't want painted is covered.

6 The points on this section of the layout had previously been weathered on another baseboard before being reclaimed for this one. Always cover the point blades for weathering of the track: normally strips of 10mm wide Tamiya masking tape over the blades will do the job. Here we have used strips of 30mm masking tape to cover the pre-weathered points.

7 Our first layer of track weathering is a simple spray over with Humbrol No. 29 from a spray can – hence the masking. It's a quick and effective means of colouring the rail sides and sleepers at the start of the ballasting process.

8 Having left the paint to dry for a couple of hours (being acrylic it goes off within 30 minutes) the rail heads need to be cleaned. It is best to do this now rather than wait until after ballasting. A couple of cleans might be necessary to get rid of all traces of paint.

9 Using a combination of Woodland Scenics fine and medium grade blended grey ballast, the two grades are mixed together in a plastic tub before application. We vary the levels of each mix to avoid the ballast looking too regimented.

10 Using fingers, we pinch ballast from the tub and drop it in place along the centre of the running line first, aiming between the sleepers. It takes time, but it is well worth investing it here to get the best looking track.

BALLASTING

11 Having completed the centres, work down the edges of the sleepers - again with your fingers - aiming for the ballast to form a neat shoulder spreading around 10-12mm away from the ends of the sleepers.

12 Next, the loose ballast needs to be tamped into place using a ½in or 1in paintbrush. This is a critical stage in ballasting – get this right and everything else will fall into place. Work along the centre of the track first, brushing loose grains of ballast off the sleepers, then work along the sleeper ends.

13 With the ballast tamped into place, it should look neat and tidy with a shoulder either side of the running lines. We've added a light covering between the running lines too and it is now ready to be glued in place.

14 In most of *Hornby Magazine's* layouts we have used PVA wood glue diluted with water to a 50:50 ratio and a drop of detergent to fix loose ballast in place, but this time we are using Deluxe Materials' Ballast Bond. This is a ready mixed adhesive formulated to work by capillary action and not to disturb loose ballast on application of the glue.

15 Place a Roket Fine Tip on top of the bottle (one is supplied with each bottle of Ballast Bond), allow the glue to flow into the fine tip and begin application down the centre of the track. As with the PVA, it will spread via capillary action. Wetting the ballast with water isn't essential, but we found a spray with a water mister did help it flow more easily.

16 With the glue applied, the ballast won't look at its best - but be patient and allow the glue to cure thoroughly before moving onto the next stage.

17 Left overnight, the glue is now set and the ballast is ready for weathering. We are going to apply basic colours at this stage, but more can be added in the future. The starting points are Geoscenics Track Grime followed by Geoscenics Black Concentrate – both let down with water to a 50:50 ratio.

18 The most effective way to apply the Geoscenics colours is with an airbrush, but it can be done by hand by letting the colours down further with 75% water and 25% colour. Here we are using an Iwata dual action airbrush to apply Track Grime.

19 The final application of Black Concentrate is made down the centre of the track helping to blend it into the original ballasting from the scenic section of this layout. This can be built up in layers until the desired level of weathering is reached, several thin coats being much more effective than one heavy attack of paint. The track now needs cleaning again once the paint has dried, then trains can start running.

SKILLS GUIDE: LAYOUT CONSTRUCTION

Building PLATFORMS

There are myriad methods and materials which can be used to make model platforms. **MIKE WILD** explains how a combination of timber, plastic, card, resin and ballast can be used to create realistic platforms to fit any location.

TOOLS & glues
- Handsaw
- Tape measure
- Steel ruler
- Pencil
- Craft knife
- Scissors
- Contact adhesive
- PVA wood glue

The *Hornby Magazine* layout Grosvenor Square boasts four separate platforms, offering seven platform faces. The surface is Slater's embossed Plastikard with mounting card, MDF and Redutex brick textures making up the underlying parts.

EVERY TIME WE CATCH A TRAIN, we use a platform. But how often have we actually taken note of how they are built? When it came to building Grosvenor Square – a seven platform terminus station, we had to develop a simple, cost effective and timely method of building platforms and, as the signature feature, they had to look right too.

There a lot of choices when it comes to model platforms. Kits, ready-made and scratchbuilding are the main options, but within that there are choices of material including timber, plastic and card. Kits can be useful but time consuming while ready-made structures are quick to install but limited in their flexibility.

For this layout, the only real option was a multi-media scratchbuilding project, using methods which should make it relatively quick to erect the seven platform faces. The basis is 12mm Medium Density Fibreboard (MDF) which is cheap to buy and easy to cut. It also gives good clean edges which is very useful for adding facing to the platform edges. However, there isn't a depth of MDF available which gives the perfect height for platforms, so we have raised the total depth to 16mm with two layers of 1/16in cork.

Edging is cut from sheets of Redutex brick sheeting – a wonderful material range which consists of ready coloured self-adhesive flexible resin sheets which can be cut to shape and applied in minutes. These have been a tremendous help in getting the base structure completed in a timely fashion.

Topping the base is 2mm thick mounting card covered with Slater's embossed Plastikard. This has been cut into strips for the edges and panels for the centres before being treated to a triple coating of paints consisting of Tamiya Medium Sea Grey, Lifecolor Rainmarks wash and Humbrol acrylic matt varnish.

The completed platforms are all capable of hosting a six coach train – two will hold six plus a parcels van – and are now ready for the finishing touches of detailing and weathering. The step by step guide explains how we built the platforms from the ground up. ■

WHAT WE USED

PRODUCT	SOURCE	CAT NO.
12mm Medium Density Fibre board	DIY store	-
1/16in cork sheet	Gaugemaster	-
2.0mm thick mounting card	Hobby store	-
Embossed Plastikard paving	Slaters	0414
Flexible embossed pre-coloured brick sheets	Redutex	076LD112
Medium Sea Grey acrylic	Tamiya	XF-83
Rain marks wash acrylic	Lifecolor	LPW11
Matt varnish	Humbrol	49
Fine blended grey ballast	Woodland Scenics	B1393
Medium blended grey ballast	Woodland Scenics	B1394

PLATFORMS

SKILLS GUIDE: LAYOUT CONSTRUCTION

STEP BY STEP: BUILDING PLATFORMS FOR GROSVENOR SQUARE

1 The basis of the platforms is 12mm MDF, but unfortunately it isn't quite the right height and 16mm MDF isn't available from stores. However, it cuts easily and is relatively cheap too. We cut strips from two 4ft x 2ft sheets to build these platforms.

2 All of the straight sections of platform and the area underneath the station building were cut to size first and laid out on the layout. Any adjustments were then made prior to the final sections for the ends and ramps being cut to length.

3 To begin raising the height of the platform base, 1/16in cork sheet was laid underneath – this was a simple, quick and effective means of achieving small height increases.

4 With a brick face positioned against the now 14mm deep platform base, trains were positioned in the platforms to gauge their height. Diagnosis: they were still too low.

Another layer of cork was layered on top of the MDF base next to add a further 2mm to the overall height of the platform bases which for us turned out to be just about perfect.

5

6 Redutex brick sheets, a self-adhesive moulded and pre-coloured resin material, were cut into 15mm deep strips to make the platform edging – a process which took a little over an hour to edge the entire platform area.

7 Next the surfaces were cut from 2mm thick mounting card taking care to ensure adequate clearance for rolling stock moving in and out of the station.

8 The overhang of the platform tops will give a realistic appearance to the finished station. Here we see it all coming together under the station canopy.

9 To create the platform edging, Slater's embossed stone Plastikard was cut into strips so that the stones could be laid along the edge of each platform. Contact adhesive secures these in place.

10 The main platform surface is formed from strips of the same stone Plastikard positioned at 90 degrees to the edging to distinguish different patterns. Each panel was cut to size with a craft knife and steel ruler.

11 Contact adhesive was used throughout this part of the build to fix the plastic sheet to the cardboard tops.

12 To allow the card to bend neatly at the ends of the platforms a triangular notch was scribed in the rear 80mm from the end.

This was then overlaid with embossed Plastikard in the same way with the plastic being scribed to follow the bend for the ramp too.

13

PLATFORMS

Suitably painted in stone grey colours and with use of Lifecolor washes the platforms are starting to look the part.

14 After several hours of cutting and shaping Plastikard, the platform surfaces were complete. To create a neat edge with the station building the Plastikard sheets go underneath the rear of the building so no joins are apparent.

Colouring starts with a thinned coat of Tamiya Medium Sea Grey acrylic (XF-83) applied by brush. It was thinned with acrylic thinners to make application quicker and easier.

Next, Lifecolour Rainmarks wash (LPW11) was brushed over the platforms and left to dry before being re-worked where necessary with the remover liquid from the Rain and Dust Liquid Pigments set.

To soften the appearance of the colours, a final application of Humbrol Matt Varnish (49) was sprayed over the platforms readying them for final weathering and detailing.

Finally the platforms were glued down to the bases using contact adhesive and the final section of the rear platform was filled with Woodland Scenics blended grey ballast secured in place with PVA glue to give this area a different look.

SKILLS GUIDE: LAYOUT CONSTRUCTION

THE ALTERNATIVES...

BUILDING PLATFORMS WITH CARD

A number of card kits exist for platforms including those produced by Metcalfe and Superquick. This kit is a Scalescenes download which was built for this simple terminus station layout. It consists of 2mm thick artists mounting board overlaid with textures cut from home printed A4 sheets. The finished model has stone facing and, while it takes some time to assemble, it goes together well and can be built to any size by printing multiple kits. Visit www.scalescenes.com to see the full range of platform kits and more. Brick finishes are available as well as stone.

Above: **The completed Scalescenes kit for a stone platform in 'OO'.**

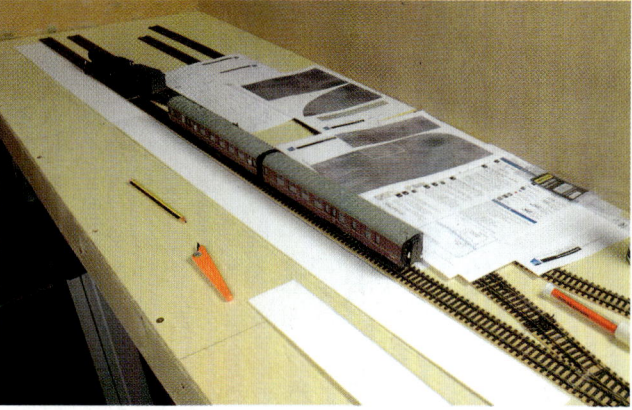

Above: **The Scalescenes kit can be printed at home and overlaid on card.**

PLATFORMS ON A CURVE

Curved platforms are amongst the hardest to build in model form. Clearances have to be checked and double checked and then there is the difficulty of choosing the right material. For *Hornby Magazine's* office test track Topley Dale, we used 12mm MDF and 3mm hardboard to make the two curved platforms for the station. The 12mm MDF base was cut to size using a paper template as a guide followed by the final surface from hardboard. To complete the modelling Wills stone sheets were cut into strips to make the edging while Woodland Scenics fine ballast makes the finishing touch for the surface. This was recoloured with Tamiya grey applied via an airbrush. Detailing followed by Ratio fencing, Hornby Skaledale benches, DCC Concepts lights and a set of Skaledale station buildings.

Trial positioning the station buildings gives a guide to where the platforms will go on Topley Dale.

PECO CONCRETE PLATFORMS

The concrete platform edging sections by Peco are ideal for Southern Region and modern layouts. For straight platforms they are simple to use, as illustrated here in the early phases of construction for Twelve Trees Junction. The sections clip together and can be glued with plastic cement such as Deluxe Materials Plastic Magic. End ramps are available too. To create the platform surface, we reinforced the edging with plastic strips cut as braces before adding plastic sheet for the tops. This was then skimmed with household filler to give the platforms a natural finish which sat level with the Peco edging. Alternatively, 2mm thick plastic sheet instead of the 1mm thick used here, can be used for the surface to avoid the need for filler.

Visit www.peco-uk.com to see the full range of platform edging.

Above: **A pencil taped to the side of a carriage marks the position of the platform edge.**

Above: **Deluxe Materials' Plastic Magic glues the plastic sheet stretchers to the edging.**

PLATFORMS

Above: Marking the position of the platform edge.

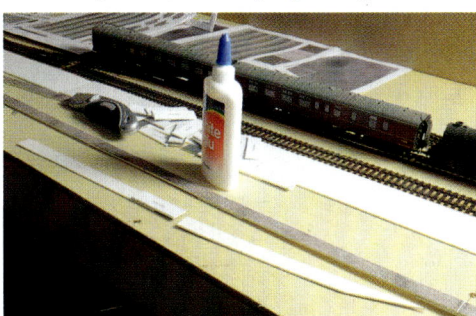
Below: PVA glue can be used to join parts together.

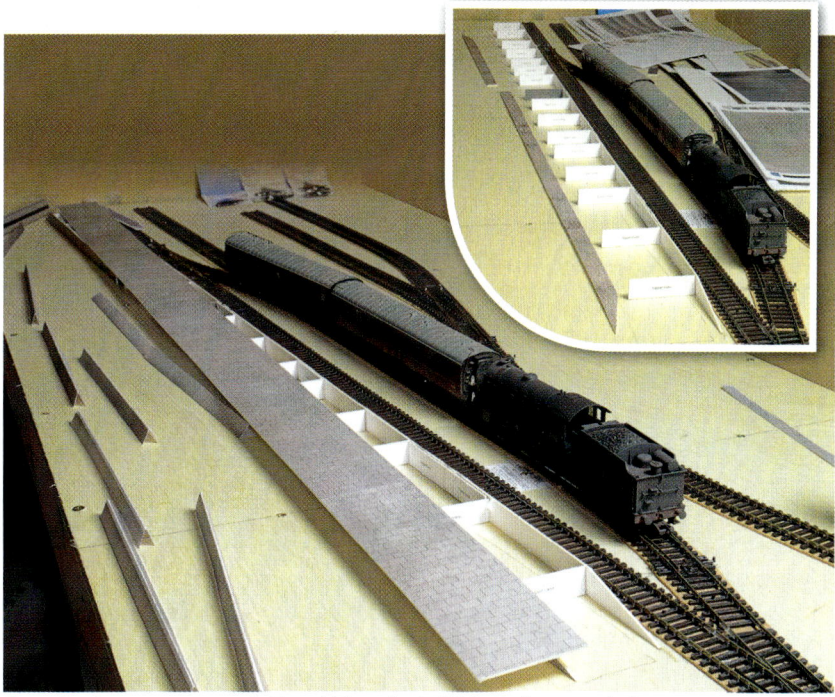
Above: Paper textures are overlaid on thick card to build the Scalescenes platform.

Above: Paper templates allow bases to be cut from 12mm MDF. Below: Wills stone plastic sheet was cut into strips for the platform faces while an airbrush was used to colour the final surface.

The MDF platform bases were cut to shape with a jigsaw using the paper templates as a guide. An important step is to check that trains will pass through without issue.

Above left: 1mm plastic sheet is used as an infill for the platform surface.

Below left: Careful masking of the track and platform edges means the final surface can be sprayed grey.

Right: A Hornby 'West Country' and six Mk 1 carriages check the platform length with accommodate the required trains.

SKILLS GUIDE: LAYOUT CONSTRUCTION

Working semaphores

Installing working semaphore signals has never been simpler thanks to the ready-made motor driven models available from Dapol. **MIKE WILD** explains how to connect the 'OO' gauge versions for both analogue and digital users.

SEMAPHORE SIGNALS

SIGNALS are an essential part of the real railway – without them disaster would unfold very quickly. In the world of model railways we often pay little attention to this essential equipment partly because of the perceived complexity of installing working semaphore signals.

Dapol's introduction of ready-made working semaphores has been very well received and we have used these products on a number of *Hornby Magazine*'s exhibition layouts, perhaps most notably on Grosvenor Square where seven GWR lower quadrant signals control departures from this seven-platform terminus station.

These signals have been developed with ease of installation in mind and they succeed in this wholly. They do, however, require care during their installation, particularly when being wired into an analogue layout as a regulated stable voltage is necessary to avoid damaging the delicate electronics inside the bases. For digital installations, life is made simpler by the fact that a specialist accessory decoder by Gaugemaster does the job for you. It should also be noted that standard accessory decoders cannot be used to operate Dapol's signals.

For this installation we have shown how a 12v regulated supply can be set up and how to install and connect the signals to a switch to operate the arms. It is all straightforward and will take around 45 minutes per signal depending upon how long the wires need to be and whether they cross baseboard joints. The more joints you have to cross, the longer it will take to install the necessary wiring.

The end result is working signals which add detail, life and realism to a model railway. Now you really can drive your trains to the signals, just like the real thing. ■

WHAT WE USED		
PRODUCT	SUPPLIER	CAT NO.
LMS motorised stop (home) signal	www.dapol.co.uk	4L-002-001
LE DC 12v/2A power supply adaptor	www.amazon.co.uk	LE DC 12V
DROK DC-DC 12v voltage regulator	www.amazon.co.uk	LM2596
Dapol semaphore accessory decoder (DCC only)	www.gaugemasterretail.com	TTSC300

A BR '3MT' 2-6-2T enters the passing loop at Ashland with a set of Maunsell carriages and passes the newly installed Dapol signal. A second signal has been installed at the end of the loop behind the camera which to controls departures in the opposite direction.

SKILLS GUIDE: LAYOUT CONSTRUCTION

SEMAPHORE SIGNALS

STEP BY STEP: INSTALLING DAPOL SEMAPHORE SIGNALS IN 'OO'

1
Dapol produces a range of single arm signals for GWR, SR and LMS style stop and distants. This is a LMS/BR stop signal which we will be installing at the end of a loop. Full instructions are supplied with each model.

2 Physical installation couldn't be simpler. A 14mm diameter hole is required through the baseboard to accommodate the mount. If you have already ballasted your track, a small amount of stone removal may be necessary to create a level mounting surface.

3 Release the wires from their packing band and unwind the securing nut to prepare the signal for installation.

4
The wires can then be threaded through the baseboard followed by the mounting base on the signal. Once in position it will sit flush and level with the baseboard surface.

5
Underneath the board, wind the securing nut back onto the threaded base to secure the signal in place. Don't over-tighten the nut as it can put strain on the mechanism – finger-tight is perfectly acceptable.

6
Next we need to prepare the connections back to the control panel for this analogue operated signal. Using a terminal block, the red, black and two yellow wires were joined on one side. The black and red were extended first back to the power source as detailed in the instruction sheet.

7
As this signal is being installed on a portable layout, the red and black cables were taken back to a plug-in terminal block which will provide a detachable power connection from the control panel. The spare terminals to the left of the red wire will be used to extend the yellow wires later.

8
Dapol's signals require a regulated voltage to ensure their safe operation, but fortunately 12v power supplies and variable regulator circuits are cheap to buy – this pair cost just £18 from Amazon.

9
The regulator we had selected required the power connections to be soldered to the board, but others have screw terminals. A connector supplied with the 12v power adapter was added to the other end of the input wires to make connection of the adapter simple.

SEMAPHORE SIGNALS

10 The regulator circuit board was fixed in position underneath the control panel. Three circuits are being run from this regulator – one for point motors and two separate circuits for the two signals on the layout. The contact points for the output have been pre-tinned ready for connection of the red and black wires from the signal.

11 To complete the circuit the red and black wires were soldered to the output terminals on the voltage regulator taking care to ensure that the polarity was correct as per Dapol's instruction sheet. Red is positive and black is negative.

12 The power adapter was then connected so that we could set the output voltage. As this regulator is being used to power both Dapol signals and DCC Concepts Cobalt point motors we set the output voltage to 9v – a safe level for both devices.

13 Having established the power source, we can now extend the yellow wires from the signal back to a push-to-make switch on the control panel. The first step is to extend the wires using the spare connections on the same terminal blocks as we used for the red and black wires.

14 Using orange cable to distinguish the wires from the power feed the switch cables were soldered to this push-to-make switch completing the circuit. Only one switch is required for each signal – each press activates the signal's motor to change the arm position.

15 A 7mm diameter hole in the control panel allows the switch to be allocated a position mirroring its location on the layout.

16 That completes installation of the analogue signal. If you wish, the base can be painted or ballasted in to blend it into the scenery of the layout. If you choose to ballast it into place, ensure you don't get glue on the operating wire.

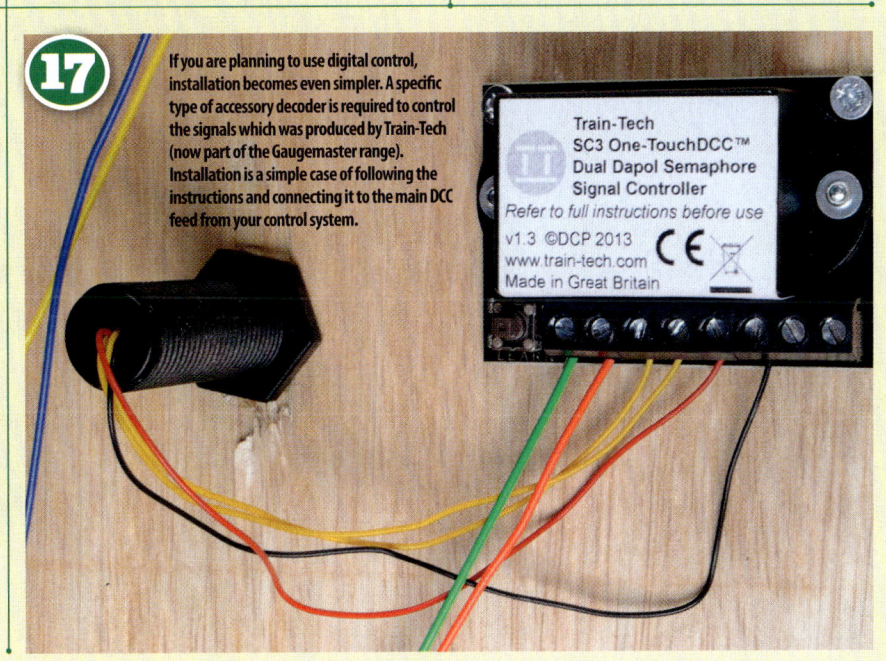

17 If you are planning to use digital control, installation becomes even simpler. A specific type of accessory decoder is required to control the signals which was produced by Train-Tech (now part of the Gaugemaster range). Installation is a simple case of following the instructions and connecting it to the main DCC feed from your control system.

SCENICS

SKILLS GUIDE: LAYOUT CONSTRUCTION

Building ROADS

The railway and road systems intersect many times over, so it is hardly surprising that many layouts include road vehicles. **MIKE WILD** presents a selection of simple solutions to build your own highways.

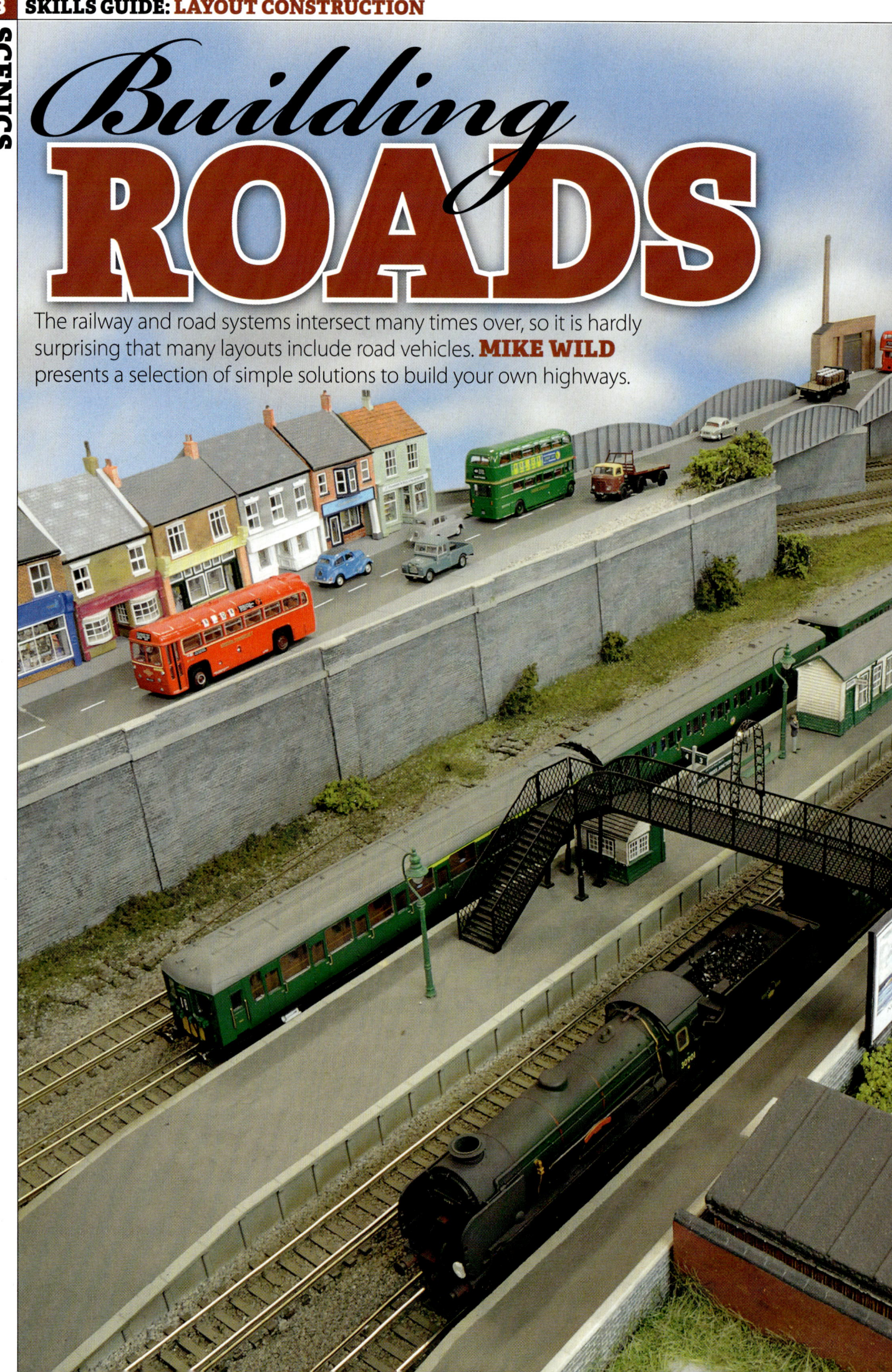

SCENICS

Below: Roadways surround our railways providing transport links from the station forecourt and goods yard into the town and surroundings. In this view of Twelve Trees Junction, there are three types of model road construction. The main road at the back is artists' card from Hobbycraft with Busch rub-on road markings, at the front right chinchilla dust is used as the ground covering around the garage and builder's yard, while the station forecourt is a skim of household filler painted grey.

Above: German scenic manufacturers Busch and Noch produce a range of self-adhesive products to create street scenes ranging from smooth asphalt to traditional cobbles as well as sheets of parking spaces and more. This is Busch's self-adhesive country road which is simple to lay and has a degree of flexibility to allow it to follow gentle curves.

ROADS come in all shapes and sizes from minor lanes to multi-lane motorways - and the chances are that you will want to add at least one form of road or another to your model railway. Just like the railway, roads need planning to make sure they will fit in with the railway scene: after all, the two transport mediums work hand in hand (so goes the theory of integrated transport).

There are many ways to produce model roads and a vast number of products on the market. Here we are providing an overview of the choices available to you, but if you want to go further there is also the possibility of introducing moving road vehicles with Faller's car system designed for 'HO' scale European outline railways.

We will concentrate on static roads here explaining the methods used across *Hornby Magazine's* exhibition layouts. These range from artists' mounting card chosen in a suitable charcoal grey base colour at the simplest end of the scale through to bespoke potholed road kits, fine ballasts and even specially designed self-adhesive products from Europe.

Whichever road you go down, always ensure you have enough space for the number of lanes you want to include and don't be tempted to overpopulate them once complete. This is particularly important on a 1960s period layout when private car ownership was just taking off.

When it comes to vehicles, the world is your oyster. With the likes of Oxford Diecast, EFE, Corgi and BT Models all producing 1:76 scale vehicles for 'OO' gauge layouts, modellers in that scale are now truly spoilt. These ranges include buses, lorries, vans, cars, tractors, diggers and more – and covering a variety of periods in motoring. An increasing range of products is becoming available for 'N' gauge too through Oxford Diecast, BT Models and Bachmann's Graham Farish brand while 'O' gauge can look to the huge range of 1:43 scale cars and light commercials that are available.

Check out the useful links panel for more suggestions to find that perfect road surface or vehicle for your layout. ■

SKILLS GUIDE: LAYOUT CONSTRUCTION

Above: Recreating the subtle effect of asphalt is a challenge in miniature, but one of the options available is Redutex textured self-adhesive sheets. These are very simple to use and realistic in their finish. Supplied in 12in x 8in sheets, they can be cut to size to suit any location. This is the station forecourt on Grosvenor Square which uses Redutex sheets for the road and paths.

Below: An ideal way of providing roads in a goods yard are stone setts such as those produced by Wills. Offered in 6in x 4in plastic sheets, they can be cut to size with a craft knife while the edging stones can be removed from the main sheet and arranged along the side of the main roadway. Set into place with ballast and static grass they make a great finishing touch to a goods yard.

USEFUL LINKS	
Geoscenics	www.geoscenics.co.uk
Redutex	www.hobby-lines.co.uk/collections/redutex
Hobbycraft	www.hobbycraft.com
Gaugemaster	www.gaugemasterretail.com
Wills	www.peco-uk.com
Noch	www.gaugemasterretail.com
Busch	www.goldenvalleyhobbies.com
Woodland Scenics	www.bachmann.co.uk
Oxford Diecast	www.oxford-diecast.co.uk
EFE	www.bachmann.co.uk
Corgi	www.corgi.com
BT Models	www.ayrey.co.uk

Above: Goods yards often had gravel yards and a simple way of replicating this is with chinchilla dust. Available from pet shops, its fine texture and buff appearance make it a perfect medium for modelling gravel yards. Alternatives include fine grade ballasts from the likes of Woodland Scenics.

SCENICS

Level crossings make an attractive feature on a model railway. This model uses Train-Tech's illuminated and sound equipped crossing lights together with artists' mounting card for the approach road and Wills planked sheets for the infill across the railway. Complete kits are available for level crossings containing barriers and track section for set track railways from Peco and Hornby too.

Above: Another alternative for a goods yard is to use air drying clay. This can be spread out over a layer of PVA glue and pressed in between the sleepers and their ends to suggest a railway bedded into the ground, as here on St Stephens Road. Air dry clay is available from Geoscenics.

Not all roads are made to a high standard with many early and minor roads having a rough finish. This can be replicated with Geoscenics' potholed road kit which contains all the ground cover materials required to recreate a realistic finish.

SKILLS GUIDE: LAYOUT CONSTRUCTION

Landscaping

NIGEL BURKIN shows how to create a model landscape with one of the cheapest and easiest methods of all.

ONE OF THE LAYOUT building tasks I particularly enjoy is creating the basic landscape. This is the process of filling in the gaps between man-made features such as the railway, roads and structures with a land surface. No matter if the landscape is to be spectacularly mountainous, rocky, rolling or relatively flat, it can be achieved using some fairly simple and inexpensive techniques.

Here, I will describe one of the cheapest and most effective ways of making landscape hard shell. A lattice of cardboard is glued together and covered in plaster-impregnated cloth.

It is a technique I regularly use to make a lightweight landscape to which scenery is applied. It can be used to span large areas between baseboard frames and the baseboard top. It's perfect for those areas where there is nothing to support foam blocks or balled-up newspaper too.

Tools of the trade

The principal tool is a hot glue gun together with standard glue sticks. Hot glue enables the assembly of a section of lattice in no time at all because of the speed at which the glue cools and hardens. The glue won't be affected by water either which is important for the covering of plaster cloth.

It is easy to burn your fingers by getting glue on them and it is difficult to remove, so wear protective gloves when using the gun. They will not protect you from the heat but are quick to remove so the glue does not continue to burn. In use, hot glue can string a little, so protect sensitive areas of the layout from the web of fine glue strings that can occur.

It takes a little dedication to create lattice hard landscaping, especially for a large layout. To begin, you must collect together as many cardboard boxes as you think you are going to need, preferably corrugated cardboard, which is stronger than single layer card. It takes a little time to tear the cardboard boxes into strips which are woven together to make the lattice structure. The width of the strips can be varied depending on the area being covered. Typically, I cut my strips between 10mm and 15mm in width and when I need strength, I cut each one along the line of the corrugations, not across them. Should you need strips that are more flexible, cut across the corrugations.

When you have a goodly bundle of strips long enough to span the widest part of the gap you need to cover with landscape, plug in the hot glue gun and make a start on gluing the vertical strips in place, secured at the top and bottom of the slope. Space them about 15mm to 25mm apart, give or take a millimetre or two. It's not an exact science and each strip is adjusted and trimmed to length to adjust the angle of slope and the depth of it.

When the vertical strips are secured in place, the horizontal ones are woven through them to create a structure strong enough to support wet »

Once hardened and dry, the plaster bandage can be stained or painted. Woodland Scenics Earth Undercoat (C1229) is used on my layout, although any diluted water based brown paint would do the job. The land behind the blue Class 09 is now ready for greenery to be added.

STEP BY STEP MAKING HARD SHELL LANDSCAPES

Beginner · Intermediate · Advanced — SKILL LEVEL

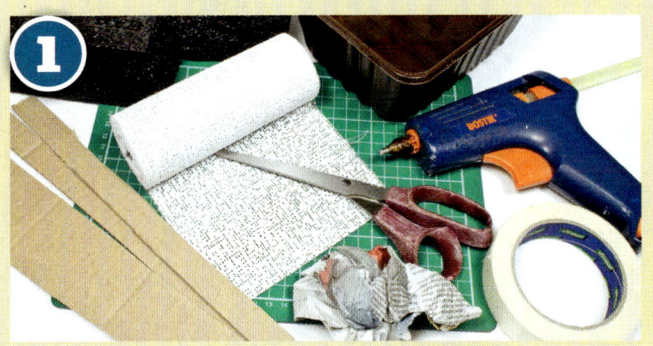

1

Hard shell landscaping can be achieved in a variety of ways. Materials suitable for supporting a layer of plaster cloth include packing foam, balled-up newspaper and of course, cardboard. A hot glue gun is an essential piece of kit for this technique and plaster cloth forms the hard surface to support the scenery.

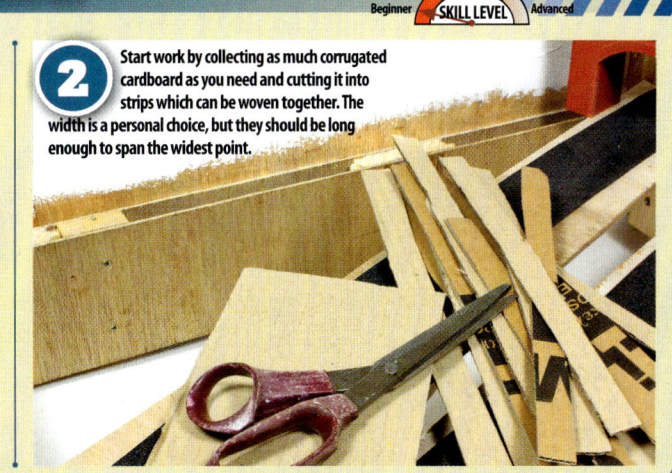

2

Start work by collecting as much corrugated cardboard as you need and cutting it into strips which can be woven together. The width is a personal choice, but they should be long enough to span the widest point.

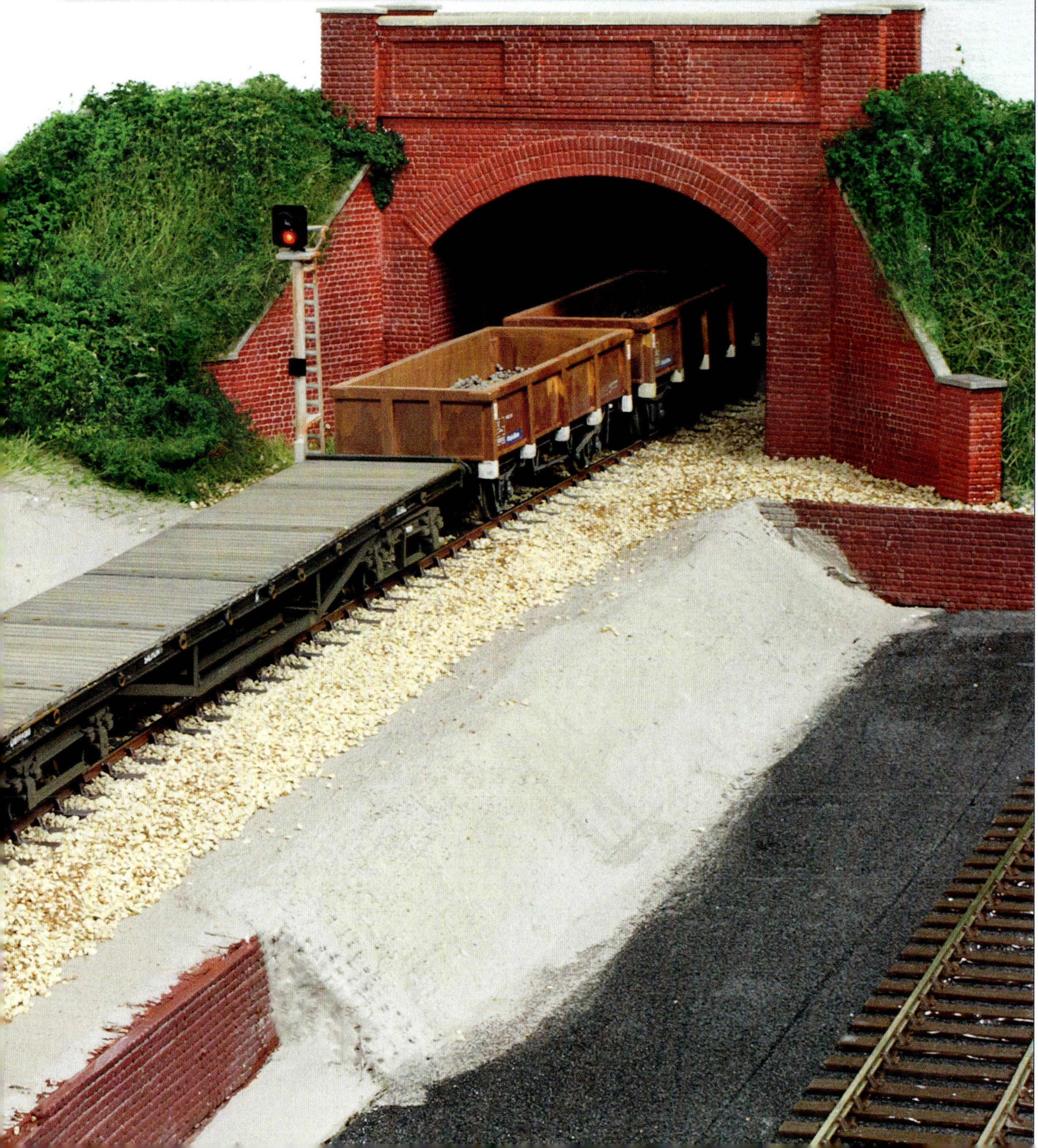

SKILLS GUIDE: LAYOUT CONSTRUCTION

STEP BY STEP: MAKING HARD SHELL LANDSCAPES

3 Hot glue is used to secure the card strips to the baseboard frame, backdrop board and track bed. It speeds the job up dramatically and is resistant to moisture from wet plaster cloth.

4 Start by applying the cross strips first (or vertical ones on a slope), secured at the ends with hot glue. Note how I have tucked the ends under the plywood forming the trackbed.

5 Thread in the long or horizontal strips of card through the vertical ones, ensuring that each strip threads above and below the vertical ones in an alternate pattern for strength.

6 Hot glue is used to secure the long card pieces to every third (or so) short or vertical strip.

7 The lattice looks neat, yet it is strong enough to support wet plaster cloth used for hard shell landscaping.

8 To prevent water from plaster cloth from soaking and weakening the card strips, masking tape is applied to the lattice in long strips until it is covered with at least two layers.

9 Managing the mess of using plaster cloth is a matter of preparing the materials and working area first. Protect adjacent track and other features with masking tape and old newspaper.

plaster cloth. Use hot glue to secure each weave of the lattice to one another. The lattice will not be strong enough at this stage to support scenery structures or your weight, so avoid leaning on it!

One of the biggest causes of failure of this technique is soggy cardboard when it falls in taking the plaster cloth with it creating a horrible mess. The secret to protecting the lattice from damp is to cover it with at least two layers of masking tape, including the extreme edges. Be sure it is pressed firmly in place before proceeding to hard shell application.

Applying the hard shell

The potential for making a complete mess should not be underestimated! Plaster cloth application is messy at the best of times. By carefully preparing your work area, most of this can be avoided. Lay out your tools and protective coverings neatly. Cut the plaster cloth into the required pieces ready for use and have some cloths to hand to wipe up any accidental spillage.

ModRoc and other brands of plaster cloth harden in a matter of a few minutes, especially when the environment is warm. Be prepared to work quickly once the plaster cloth is wet - hence the importance of logically setting out your work area. Soak only as much as you need at a time and transfer it to the working area after the excess moisture has been removed by squeezing against the water dish. Pop it into place and smooth down with your fingers to remove the tiny holes as far as possible. Do not overwork it once it begins to set.

As the layers are built up, the plaster cloth will harden and you will get a feel for how much is needed for your application. I usually apply two to three layers for a small span and up to five for a wide span of landscaping. Avoid the temptation to poke or prod it once the job is done. When finished, walk away, clean up your tools and the working area and leave the hard shell for several days to harden and cure.

Setting the scene

It is tempting to think that hard shell is ready to paint after it has first hardened. Ideally, the it should be left to dry out for several days depending on the conditions. There is a simple test to see if your hard shell is ready for paint: touch it with the palm of your hand and if it feels 'cold' to the touch, it is still holding moisture. When that cold feeling has gone, it is ready for paint.

Painting seals the hard shell ready for addition of scenic materials and will prevent white from showing through. Some modellers use household paints diluted a little so it soaks into the hard shell. Woodland Scenics brown coloured C1229 Earth Undercoat pigment can be applied undiluted to the hard shell where it will soak into the plaster.

Plaster cloth and lattice hard shell is surprisingly strong and can be used to span quite large areas without support. However, it does have its limitations and it may be necessary to add some support to the underside of the lattice if it appears to want to sag under its own weight. With the hard shell completed, it can be treated with rock moulds, skimmed with casting plaster to add to the relief or textured with turf, static grass, bushes, shrubs and more.

The real benefit of the technique is its relative cheapness and today when modelling budgets are under particular stress, low cost methods for layout building and scenery are worth considering and will allow more money to be spent on quality scenery materials for a great looking layout. ■

10 Dip the plaster cloth quickly in water, but do not soak it! Allow excess water to drain from it before placing on the masking tape.

TIP Using plaster cloth can be a messy process. Make sure you cover your working area with newspaper and also mask areas of previously completed scenery and track to stop any unwanted plaster marks.

11 I find it easier to use plaster cloth in small strips which ensures that none of it hardens before it can be used. Nonetheless, careful but speedy application is a must, especially if your plaster cloth has a short setting time.

12 Smooth the plaster cloth with fingers to hide all those tiny holes and to create a smooth surface. At least three layers are needed for a fixed layout and more for a portable one where durability is important.

13 The stages of hard shell landscaping are demonstrated in this picture. Masking tape covers the card lattice protecting it from the plaster cloth application until it completely dries. A coat of brown or earth-coloured paint is applied to the dry hard shell to prepare it for scenery application which can include static grass, turf, shrubs and bushes. Surrounding features are protected with masking tape when plaster cloth is applied.

SKILLS GUIDE: LAYOUT CONSTRUCTION

SCENICS

Static grass *essentials*

Static grass is a great way of creating realistic scenery. **NIGEL BURKIN** demonstrates how to apply static grass and suggests some simple enhancements.

SCENICS

Static grass makes a huge difference to the appearance of a scenic model railway. The grass alongside the track on *Hornby Magazine's* Axe Regis layout is static grass detailed with fine and coarse turfs as well as multiple layers of static fibres.

SCENERY MODELLING has long moved away from coloured sawdust to represent grass and weeds. Even dyed ground foam scatter has taken a back seat to the growing popularity of static grass which is available from a number of manufacturers and in a variety of natural colours ranging from the bright to the subtle.

Static grasses are simple to use. They are scattered onto the landscape surface after coating with either scenery adhesive or diluted PVA glue. A special electric applicator is used to charge the grasses with static electricity, enabling the grasses to stand upright in the adhesive in a natural looking way.

Static grass applicators can be expensive to buy depending on the model, but the results speak for themselves and the devices are similarly priced to a new locomotive. The upside is that they produce grass which matches the detailing of the locomotives which we can now buy ready-to-run.

Static grass is produced in a variety of lengths from 1mm to 6mm depending on the manufacturer. MiniNatur offers an 'Early Fall' and 'Late Fall' colour in various lengths which works well for dry summer grasses in the context of British landscape modelling. Static grass is also produced by Green Scene, Noch, Woodland Scenics and War World Scenics.

Applying static grass

Firstly, protect the track, ballast and any lineside features from spray adhesive and grass fibres with masking tape and newspaper. Damp paper towels will protect buildings and structures from stray fibres which can be the very devil to remove – glue or no glue! Backdrop boards are covered in newspaper for the same reason.

The Noch applicator I use is supplied with a variety of screens and a narrow funnel. Before selecting a screen, the applicator is filled to about one third with static grass material teased out so it is loose. I usually use a fine mesh screen fitted to the end of the applicator, as demonstrated in the photographs, when working on larger areas. For smaller or more confined areas, the mesh screen can be replaced with the funnel which directs the static grass to where it is needed. Typically, working on a 2ft square area of landscape at a time, unless treating awkward spots, is a good policy.

An essential first step is a scattering of green or blended green 'Fine Turf' by Woodland Scenics as an undercoat onto the hard shell to disguise the painted hard shell before the first layer of grass is applied when lush growth is needed. Grasses can be applied directly to the hard shell, especially if thin grass over soil or compacted ground is the desired effect. Be sure to achieve the right ground colour and texture first.

To prepare for the static grass fibres thinned PVA glue or Scenic Cement is spread/sprayed on to the painted hard shell before charging up the applicator. The Noch applicator relies on a grounding pin which is inserted into the wet area before the grass is sprinkled from the applicator onto the landscape. Hold the applicator an inch or two from the surface and listen for the ticking noise of the fibres leaving the applicator and hitting the landscape surface.

Remove protective materials before the glue hardens completely. Once the glue has dried, the grass fibres should be standing upright. When longer grasses are needed, apply more protection to layout features if necessary and scatter a second layer of grass. Firm hold hairspray or acrylic matt varnish can be used to hold any second application. This can be done in patches or evenly across the treated area for variety.

When you have developed your technique, remember to take a record of the exact process, including products and colours so you can repeat the process in the future. ■

ADDING TEXTURE

Some of the most effective scenery has been created using a mixture of materials and techniques which adds texture and prevents unnatural-looking uniformity. Here's a summary of possibilities:

- Add a second hit of static grass to create texture and depth
- Mix fibres of different sizes in the applicator
- Mix different colours and makes of static grass for variety
- A second application of short fibres could be of yellow or 'dry' grasses representing the longer grasses with seed heads which dry out in summer and autumn whilst the lower part of the grasses remains green
- Brush your fingers gently through some areas of grass to make them look flattened after heavy rain or strong wind. Grasses which all stand uniformly upright do not look convincing
- Sprinkle a pinch of fine turf material onto the grass in a random manner to represent weeds growing through the grass
- Summer flowers can be represented by using Woodland Scenics T48 'Flowers' scatter which includes red, white and yellow suitable for many British wild flowers

SKILLS GUIDE: LAYOUT CONSTRUCTION

STEP BY STEP: STATIC GRASS TECHNIQUES

1 Static grasses usually end up where you do not want them! Protect track, ballast and scenic details with masking tape and newspaper. Cover trees and structures with damp paper towels.

2 One option is to apply an underlying layer of fine ground foam scatter before scattering static fibres. Note how the backdrop boards have been covered in newspaper to protect them from scenery glue.

3 Dilute PVA wood glue is brushed onto the landscape surface for the first layer of scenery materials. Static grass could be directly applied to this if desired, but the base colour of the landscape will show through.

4 I prefer to apply a layer of fine turf by Woodland Scenics first. It is left to dry before spraying on a coat of scenic cement or matte medium for the static grass.

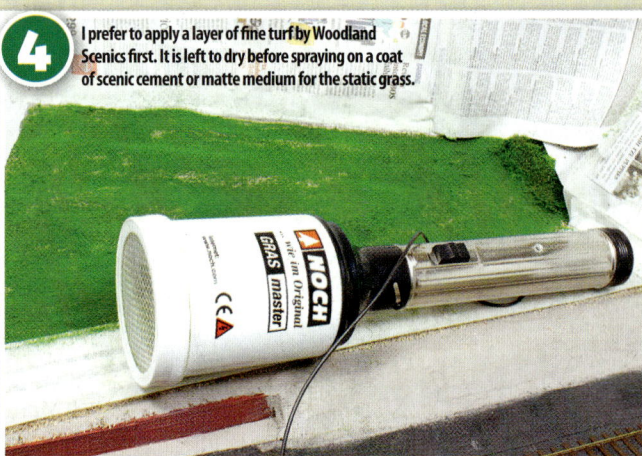

Static grasses are ideal for bedding buildings and structures into the ground such as in this shed scene at Axe Regis. Note the additional textures of fine turfs which have been added to the basic grass after application.

SCENICS

5 Load up the applicator with static grass material, mixing colours and length for variety. If the material is balled, as seen in this picture, take a few minutes to tease it out.

6 The applicator is turned on and the fibres discharged from a height of an inch or two. Note the grounding lead to the left.

7 Spray on more scenic cement or dilute matte medium to further secure the grasses if necessary. A second application of grass could be made at this stage before the glue sets.

8 Texture can be added before the glue completely dries by sprinkling some fine scatter onto the surface of the grasses to represent weeds. Coloured scatter, when applied very sparingly, gives the impression of wild flowers such as poppies.

9 Carefully remove the protective masking tape before the scenery glue completely dries out and make any minor repairs to the edge of the grassy area.

10 Static grass has grown in popularity in recent years, despite the relatively high price of electric applicators. The uniformity of static grass can be broken up using pinches of fine ground foam scatter to add the impression of weeds and flowers.

SKILLS GUIDE: LAYOUT CONSTRUCTION

Simple TREES

Making your own trees is a cost effective and therapeutic means of adding foliage to your layout. **NIGEL BURKIN** explains two methods for the DIY tree maker.

TREES CAN BE RATHER LARGE. Even the weed trees that grow on railway embankments and abandoned railway land can reach considerable height and width when left to grow unchecked. In the past, when steam power dominated the railways, trees were carefully cut back from embankments and cuttings to reduce the risk of fires and to keep railway property tidy before they became too large.

Layout builders should see trees differently. They make great scenic features, visually powerful backdrops, may be used as scenic breaks and even be used as a sort of visual sleight of hand to hide the join between structures, backscene boards and landscaping, making the layout appear finished. Taking the time to make your own trees is rewarding and enjoyable, so it is worth factoring them into your design from the very start.

Trees can be modelled in a number of ways and they are relatively easy to do for any scale. They can be used to populate embankments and cuttings and by varying their height they can add a great deal of depth to even the shallowest of layouts.

Sea foam trees

The first technique we will show here is the use of sea foam which produces ideal nondescript background trees. Sea foam is a natural plant material and the part used in tree-making and scenery is the flower. It has to be dried before use and the flower heads are delicate and easily broken which should be a consideration when using it on a portable layout. However, the natural shape and relative low cost per finished tree are factors in its favour. Considerable areas of layout can be covered with one box of sea foam and a modest outlay in scenery glue, foliage material and paint.

Sort through the box of sea foam armatures to find those most suited to tree making. Choose them according to size, shape and avoid those with excessive curl. Set up a hanging line from which the armatures can be suspended using clamps and set out a working area on a table top with suitable protective covers.

After trimming away any leaves from the armature and shaping it by cutting off unwanted branches, dip each one into a jug of dilute matte medium (an artist's varnish) for a few minutes at a time. Shake off excess matte medium and attach them to the line by the stem so they are suspended upside down. Attach a clamp or clothes pegs to the bottom end to apply weight. This will straighten them as the matte medium dries.

The armatures are left for at least 12 hours in good conditions to thoroughly dry before being painted the desired trunk and branch colour. I chose a dark brown acrylic paint sprayed on to save time.

Again, leave the armatures sufficient time to dry after painting before applying foliage material. Whilst I use ground foam from Woodland Scenics for foliage there are numerous ways of decorating sea foam trees. Noch offers a leaf product that can be applied to prepared tree armatures and this is available in several colours including summer greens – perfect for sea foam trees.

To avoid damaging the delicate armatures, I used firm hold hairspray as an adhesive. Woodland Scenics Scenic Cement could be applied too using a spray bottle instead if you prefer. To make sure the foliage material sticks well, do not be too sparing with the adhesive you choose to use - spray on a good coating.

Woodland Scenics armatures

Woodland Scenics offers a variety of tree kits, ranging from the Learning Kit (Cat No. LK953) which contains foliage, adhesive, a mix of »

TOOLS

SEA FOAM TREES
» Plastic jug or water bottle
» Plastic trays
» Bulldog clips
» Clothes pegs
» Scissors
» Tweezers
» Cocktail sticks

WOODLAND SCENICS TREES
» Brown, bauxite and grey acrylic paints for painting tree armatures
» Woodland Scenics Hob-e-Tac adhesive
» Plastic trays to hold and catch scenery material during foliage application
» Old newspapers to protect working areas

WHAT WE USED – SEA FOAM TREES	
PRODUCT	PURPOSE
Woodland Scenics S191 Scenic Cement	To soak trees
Woodland Scenics S192 Scenic Sprayer	Applying scenic cements
Brown and grey acrylic paints	Painting tree trunks
Woodland Scenics T64 medium green turf	Summer foliage
Woodland Scenics T63 light green turf	Accent colour
Extra firm hold hairspray	Scenic adhesive
Sea foam tree armatures	Tree materials

Sea foam trees dominate the background of this overhauled section of scenery. The new trees have been produced using the methods described in the step by step guide for sea foam.

SCENICS

www.keymodelworld.com

STEP BY STEP: MAKING TREES FROM SEA FOAM

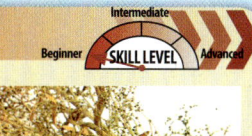
SKILL LEVEL: Beginner / Intermediate / Advanced

1
Sea foam trees are widely available from a number of sources including Noch and Woodland Scenics. A box contains enough to cover a considerable area of landscape and the smaller pieces can be used to make shrubs and bushes.

2
Basic modelling materials are all that are required. One of my favourite adhesives for applying foliage to trees and bushes is firm-hold hairspray.

3
The part of the sea foam plant used for scenery making is the flower head, suitably dried.

4
Some leaves are cut from the sea foam armature with scissors. Trim unwanted branches and cut larger pieces to the desired height.

5
Toughen the armatures by dipping them in dilute matte medium or neat Scenic Cement, long enough for it to soak in.

USEFUL LINKS

Green Scene (sea foam, forest in a box)	www.green-scenes.co.uk
Woodland Scenics	www.bachmann.co.uk
Gaugemaster (Noch products)	www.gaugemaster.com

SKILLS GUIDE: LAYOUT CONSTRUCTION

deciduous and evergreen tree armatures and full instructions to 'Realistic Tree Kits' which contain armatures and suitable foliage materials and lead-free cast metal tree kits including forest kits. Together with the wide range of foliage materials available from Woodland Scenics and other suppliers, you can have hours of fun making up trees for your layout quickly and economically.

The basis of the Woodland Scenics tree kits and armature packs is to twist flat mouldings into the desired three-dimensional shape, with branches arranged to suit. The learning kits and 'Realistic Tree Kits' contain foliage and plastic armatures, complete with a moulded base, the use of which is optional. The armature is gripped in the hands and twisted around to distribute the branches evenly around the trunk. Some branches can be removed to create different looking trees.

Woodland Scenics plastic armatures are pre-coloured and can be used without having to paint them to save time. However, painting the trees before adding foliage adds individual character and removes the plastic shine. Particular tree trunk colours can be introduced such as the reddish brown of evergreen trees, the silvery grey of trees representing beeches and the off-white trunks of birches, the ever present tree of old railway land.

Ready to plant

Having assembled a batch of trees we can now move on to plant them on a model railway.

Use the best specimens at the front and take the more nondescript designs to the back of a scene. There they will add depth to the foliage and create a perception of the trees going into the distance. It takes practice and adjustment to get them into the right place, but it is highly rewarding to reach the final stages.

The step by step guides explain the processes involved in making sea foam and Woodland Scenics trees. ■

WHAT WE USED – WOODLAND SCENICS TREES		
PRODUCT	MANUFACTURER	CAT NO.
Hob-e-Tac adhesive	Woodland Scenics	S195
Flowers	Woodland Scenics	T48
Dark green foliage	Woodland Scenics	F53
Light green turf	Woodland Scenics	T63
Medium green turf	Woodland Scenics	T64
Poly fibre	Woodland Scenics	FP178
Light green leaves	Noch	GM156
Medium green leaves	Noch	GM157

Commercial tree products come in all shapes and sizes. Woodland Scenics offers a comprehensive range of armature packs, kits and learning packs. Ready-made trees can also be improved and customised using the products and techniques described here.

STEP BY STEP: MAKING TREES FROM SEA FOAM

6 Armatures are suspended from a line whilst drying. A weight is applied to them to help straighten them while the matte medium dries.

7 After painting, the armatures are either dipped in matte medium, scenic cement or sprayed with hairspray before being rolled in foliage material.

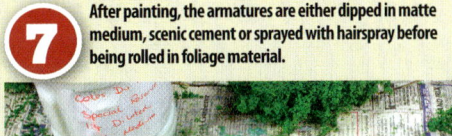

8 Woodland Scenics coarse turf makes good foliage material for '00' gauge. Leaves are available from Noch to create the same effect.

9 Using sea foam a large batch of trees can be produced quickly to develop the scenery of a layout. Build up a stock pile and then use them across your layout to their best effect, moving them around before gluing them in place.

10 With the new sea foam trees planted, the join between the landscape and the vertical backscene board is disguised to good effect.

STEP BY STEP: HOW TO MAKE PLASTIC DECIDUOUS TREES

A The LK953 tree learning kit supplies the foliage and plastic armatures for creating simple but effective trees suitable for '00' gauge layouts. The kit also includes evergreen and deciduous tree armatures and Hob-e-Tac adhesive too.

B Woodland Scenics offers packs of deciduous tree armatures of varying heights to suit various scales which are also supplied in the learning kit.

C Each armature is cleaned of moulding flash and twisted into shape using your fingers.

D Fine nose pliers help with adjusting individual branches. The twisting process should only take about five minutes per tree.

E After a coat of paint, the branches are coated in a tacky scenery adhesive. Deluxe Materials Scatter Grip adhesive is a good alternative to Hob-e-Tac.

F Rather than add individual pads of foliage, I used Poly Fibre to create complete tree canopies. It is teased out to make a fine covering.

G The Poly Fibre is sprayed with firm hold hairspray (or other spray adhesive designed for scenery work) taking care not to soak the tree stem or branches. It helps to hold the tree upside down over newspaper when applying spray glues.

H Foliage scatter is gently sprinkled onto the canopy with a tray underneath to catch the excess. A couple of layers separated with applications of spray adhesive may be required to complete this process making the tree ready to plant on your layout.

SKILLS GUIDE: LAYOUT CONSTRUCTION

DIGITAL COMMAND CONTROL

Downsizing
Building Twelvemill Bridge

What is it like building a layout in a scale that's new to you? **MIKE WILD** describes the development of new 'TT:120' layout Twelvemill Bridge.

One of the joys of railway modelling is that you are always free to change. You might have finished yet another 'OO' gauge branch line and then decide that your next project is going to be modern image 'O'. You might be half-way through your magnum opus dream loft layout and then decide that portable micro-layouts is what you want after all.

Change is ok because there are always new modelling worlds to explore.

One of the driving forces is the wealth of new ready-to-run models that are available – and seeing a new model often is the catalyst for building a new layout.

New technology means that 'N' gauge models are now as reliable and refined as their 'OO' counterparts. 'O' gauge has undergone a similar revolution and you can now buy quality models for not much more than a top of the line equivalent in a smaller scale.

On top of that, manufacturers continue to explore new avenues. As we've already explored, there's now a wealth of RTR models in 'OO9' and Dapol's sister company Lionheart has produced the first RTR models in 'O-16.5'. And then, in 2022, Hornby spearheaded the return of 'TT' with its range – supported by the likes of Peco – of 'TT:120' models.

There really has been no better time to try something new.

However, switching between scales is not as straightforward as it might appear.

Let's say you're a long-time 'OO' gauge modeller who fancies modelling in 'N'. You will need to bear in mind that while the range of 'N' gauge RTR models is bigger than it has ever been, there are still some significant gaps. You might be able to find a specific type of coach in 'OO' but there's a good change it won't exist in 'N'.

The same is true when it comes to accessories. To list all the available accessories in 'OO' would result in something like a telephone directory (remember them?!). The 'N' gauge equivalent is likely to be much smaller.

The tension lock is the default 'OO' gauge coupling. It's far from perfect but you can use it on shunting layouts. If you're moving down to 'N', you're probably going to have to rule out shunting layouts and go for a tail-chaser with long trains as the 'N' gauge coupling is better suited for this type of operation.

This may sound as though we're trying to disparage 'N' gauge. Not at all! What we're trying to illustrate is that to switch from one scale to another requires a change of mindset.

To explore what it's like to embark on a project using a scale that's new to you, we decided to build a layout in 'TT:120'.

Let's see how we got on…

Planning

The overall idea for the layout was simple – to show as many product ranges available for the new scale as possible while creating a realistic

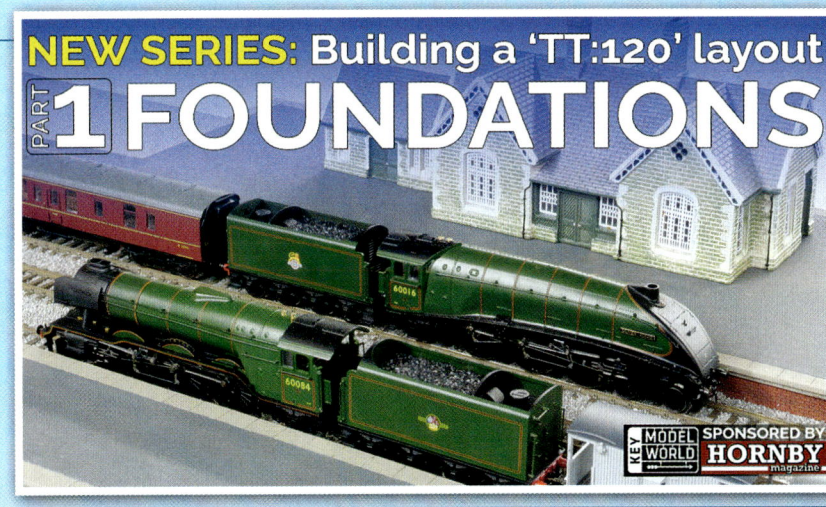

NEW SERIES: Building a 'TT:120' layout
PART 1 FOUNDATIONS
SPONSORED BY Hornby magazine

BRAND-NEW VIDEO BUILD SERIES ONLINE NOW!

Visit www.keymodelworld.com/buildingatt120modelrailway to watch our full four-part video series following construction of Twelvemill Bridge. In Part 1 we build the baseboards and platforms, and lay the track to create a working layout ready for the start of scenery, in Part 2 we detail creation of the landscape, Part 3 focuses on ground cover while Part 4 is all about the detail. Part 1 is free to watch on Key Model World and YouTube, Part 2 is free to watch with a Member account on Key Model World and Parts 3 and 4 require a Key Model World Premium Subscription. Visit www.keymodelworld.com/subscribe-today for full details.

One of the hallmarks of a successful model railway is not being able to tell what the gauge and scale it is in a photograph. Can you tell that Twelvemill Bridge is built to 'TT:120'. Find out how we built it.

SKILLS GUIDE: LAYOUT CONSTRUCTION

Hornby launched 'TT:120' with new ready-made resin buildings (under its Skaledale brand). Twelvemill Bridge uses a Skaledale station building, signalbox and goods shed. There's no specific range of 'TT:120' range of trees; you can still your favourite tree suppliers. Those on the rising ground behind the station are from Primo Models (www.primomodels.co.uk). **Mike Wild.**

setting which could fit into a spare room. The size limit was set at 10ft x 6ft to provide space for a station, goods yards, engine shed, main line double track running plus the intention of a large viaduct scene.

We devised a trackplan that would combine all the features we wanted. Planning also required consideration as to how the baseboards would be built and particularly the viaduct scene which would need to be lower than the rest of the layout. In total, six 4ft x 2ft boards were assembled using the same techniques on p202-3.

The lower boards for the viaduct were set with their tops 144mm lower than the main boards with a separate trackbed being added on timber supports to keep the track level throughout.

Choosing track laying

When it came to the track for this layout we had two choices: Hornby's sectional track system for the new scale or Peco's collection of fine scale Code 55 rail profile products. Both are to the same 12mm gauge but Hornby's track uses Code 80 rail which is a slightly larger profile than Peco's Code 55.

The finer rail profile gives a more realistic look to the finished layout while the use of flexible track means that curves can be flowed to any radius required to meet the layout design. It also means that there will be less rail joints around the full circuit, but using flexible track does require a little more work to join it altogether.

If we were to use the Hornby sectional track, every piece comes pre-fitted with metal rail joiners which makes them a simple job to slot together. With flexible track from Peco rail joiners have to be bought separately and then fitted to the ends of each section. On the positive side, the flexible track can be cut to length to suit specific layout designs whereas sectional track restricts layout designs to fixed pieces.

Another big positive for our layout build was the opportunity to use Peco's Unifrog points. These are the latest generation points from Peco which are supplied with the central crossing vee – the frog – unpowered. Out of the box, they behave like an insulated frog point whereby the vee is unpowered, but long wheelbase locomotives will run through these crossings without any issue. However, short

The landscape was made from polystyrene blocks, glued together with PVA glue and shaped with a hot wire foam cutter and covered in plaster bandage. Woodland Scenics' range is still ideal for use in 'TT:120' We built the greenery up in layers: Woodland Scenics fine blended green turf was applied, followed by layers of Green Scene and Woodland Scenics static grasses (using the Woodland Scenics Static Grass King applicator). The hedges and buses are also from Woodland Scenics. Mike Wild.

SKILLS GUIDE: LAYOUT CONSTRUCTION

DIGITAL COMMAND CONTROL

Given the 12mm track gauge of 'TT:120', we opted for Woodland Scenics' finest grade of blended ballast for Twelvemill Bridge, the same choice if we were building an 'N' gauge layout. The ballasting technique was similar to that described on p74-77: we weathered the track with Humbrol 29 aerosol, laid the granules loose and sealed them with SBR adhesive for a strong a permanent hold. The only thing we did differently was to omit the cork underlay. **Mike Wild.**

Twelvemill Bridge is a portable layout and each baseboard joint was fitted with a pair of Modeltech Pro-Track Rail Aligners (www.modeltech.uk). These are fitted in place of the final three-four sleepers at each baseboard joint and are pinned to the baseboard prior to being soldered to the underside of the rails. Once in place they firmly hold the track in place. **Jonathan Newton.**

EXCLUSIVE KITS AVAILABLE NOW!

Key Publishing has partnered with PJM Models to offer a series of new and exclusive laser-cut kits for 'TT:120'. The range comprises Great Northern Railway tunnel portals, platforms and – due imminently - a Great Northern Railway signalbox. Visit www.keymodelworld.com/shop for full details.

Z PJM specialises in producing bespoke laser-cut kits but it does have a range of kits to buy. You can see the range at www.pjmmodels.co.uk or, alternatively, contact PJM at contact@pjmmodels.co.uk to discuss your requirements.

wheelbase locomotives like the Hornby Class 08 would stall on them, but happily the points are pre-fitted with a frog switching wire which can be passed through the baseboard and connected to either a dedicated frog switch or if you are using DCC point motors with a frog switching option this can be used to change the polarity of the frog as the points change. It sounds complicated like that, but once you have done one it will feel much simpler. (You can see more about fitting point motors on p70-73).

The Peco 'TT:120' track range currently consists of medium and short radius points as well as diamond crossings. Plain yard lengths of flexible track are readily available together with matching metal and insulated rail joiners – the latter only really need to be used with analogue control layouts.

For this layout, we opted to lay the track direct onto the baseboard rather than using underlay. The smaller track didn't feel like it needed the same ballast shoulder treatment as a 'OO' gauge layout (see p74-77).

Track laying

We started to lay track on the viaduct side of the layout, working towards the station scene. This would provide the opportunity

SKILLS GUIDE: LAYOUT CONSTRUCTION

to learn how the track responded to curving and pinning. Peco's 12mm gauge track is very similar to its Code 55 9mm 'N' gauge track, where part of the rail is 'buried' in the sleepers. This does make the track strong but it makes it a little harder to bend.

The most complex part of the track plan was assembling the loops and points through the station. To ensure everything was positioned correctly, we built the PJM Models laser-cut platform kits first, using them to guide track laying.

The station features three tracks with a loop on the outer circuit against the platform, a central fast line on the outer circuit and a single line through the inner circuit platform. To provide additional train storage, a pair of long sidings were added to the inner circuit which would allow the equivalent of a six-coach train to be stored off the main circuit so that at least four full trains can be on track at any time.

'N' gauge is perfect for depicting 'trains in the landscape' and we wanted to see if 'TT:120' would share these properties. Therefore, it was designed it looked like the railway had been carved through the landscape, rather than the other way around – even though that was essentially how the layout would be built.

The advantage of the dropped board design on the viaduct side of the layout was that the

Oxford Diecast has developed a new range of suitable road vehicles for 'TT:120', including this Land Rover and Morris 1000 van. Future developments include everything from an original Mini to a Ferguson tractor and a Routemaster bus. The coal staithes are from MS Models (www.msmodels.co.uk). Mike Wild.

The current range of detailing items for 'TT:120' is small but growing rapidly. We used laser-cut platform kits by PJM Models, Scale Model Scenery fencing and Hornby Skaledale buildings on Twelvemill Bridge. Osborns Models is just one of a number of organisations producing 'TT:120' buildings whilst Gaugemaster can now offer suitable people and platform lights. **Mike Wild.**

This farm scene was created using a cottage and barn from MS Models and 3D printed vehicles from Replitek. The ground cover was made using Humbrol Smart Mud, a new material that is ready to apply direct from pot and adds realistic textures to the ground. **Mike Wild.**

landscape could fall below the level of the railway and then rise above it to suggest a rolling hills scene. The viaduct board called for a multi-level scene with the railway at the top, a road flowing down hill and under the second arch followed by a river at the lowest point passing beneath the fifth arch to create an attractive scene.

Twelvemill Bridge is now a complete layout, but one which will continue to develop with the arrival of new products for this enticing new scale. When we built it, the range of ready-to-run 'TT:120' models was limited. We used what was then available: 'A3' and 'A4' 4-6-2s, Mk 1 coaches and Pullman cars from Hornby and a selection of wagons and vans from Peco. Remember what we said earlier about other scales not having the breadth that's available in 'OO'?

However, both Hornby and Peco are promising more models and Twelvemill Bridge has hosted samples of Hornby's forthcoming 'TT:120' HST and Class 50 in recent months.

What did we think of switching to 'TT:120'? Well, we can see a bright future for it, for starters. It's been billed as the perfect compromise between 'N' and 'OO' and we can see why it's a great choice for a model railway and one which will be easier to fit into the average spare room while creating an impressive scene. ■

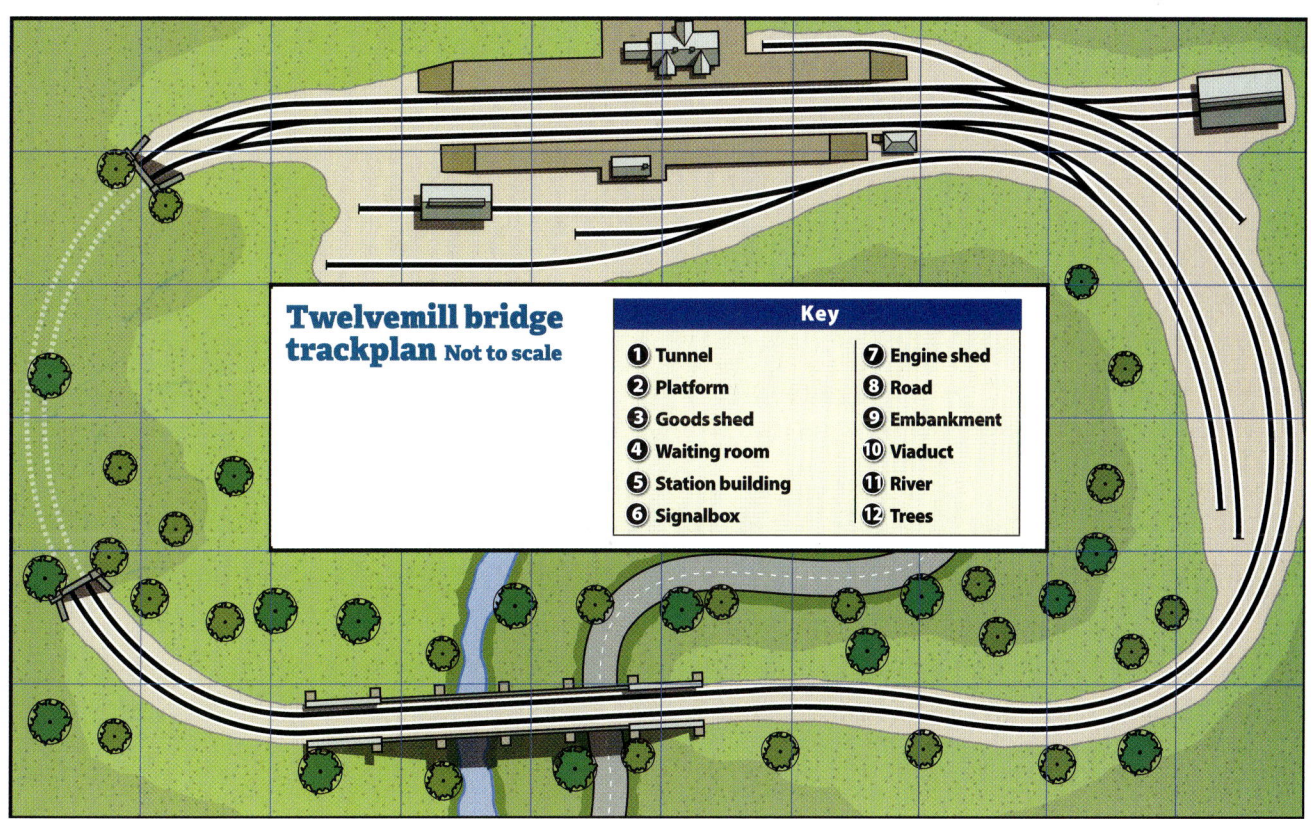

Twelvemill bridge trackplan Not to scale

Key
1. Tunnel
2. Platform
3. Goods shed
4. Waiting room
5. Station building
6. Signalbox
7. Engine shed
8. Road
9. Embankment
10. Viaduct
11. River
12. Trees

SKILLS GUIDE: LAYOUT CONSTRUCTION

LIGHTING

Woodland Scenics
JUST-PLUG SYSTEM

Lighting buildings used to be a challenge involving a range of skills, but Woodland Scenics has changed all that with its Just-Plug lighting system. **MIKE WILD** shows how bring a layout to life after dark.

This is Twelve Trees Junction, where a 'Warship' has just arrived with an Exeter-Waterloo working while a 2-EPB pauses in the platform behind. The buildings have been lit with Woodland Scenics' Just-Plug range of lighting accessories.

ADDING LIGHTING to buildings used to be difficult, involving lots of soldering and grain-of-wheat bulbs. That's no longer the case, thanks to Woodland Scenics' Just-Plug lighting system. As the name suggests, Just-Plug is a a plug-and-play lighting system that covers all the main elements needed to install interior lighting in miniature buildings and more.

Traditionally lighting of buildings could be time consuming and doubtless put modellers off from including this atmospheric addition to their layouts. Just-Plug takes all the complication out of making lighting circuits.

To illustrate how to use this product range we went to town on the station and high street buildings on *Hornby Magazine's* Twelve Trees Junction layout. The complete installation features 26 lights from the Just-Plug series. These are linked to the specially designed Light Hubs – each of which can power four LEDs and feature dimmer switches for each output – which in turn are connected to Expansion Hubs which connect the mains power supply to further Expansion Hubs and four Light Hubs from each Expansion Hub. It may sound complicated but it really is a very simple system – see Diagram 1 on page 116.

Moreover, it doesn't stop at just the lighting circuits themselves. It covers specific kits for blacking out the interior of buildings, window films to improve the performance of interior lights – and to tint the windows too – a very handy Tidy Wire Kit which does exactly what it says. Plus, while we have used the warm white LEDs for our project, there are a number of other lighting colours available in the range.

To complete our scene we added station lamps and street lamps using the DCC Concepts swan neck lamp range, which is now part of the Gaugemaster range. Using the value packs – each of which contains six full height lamps, two wall mounted lamps, a pack of LEDs and miniature circuit boards to connect the lamps to a 9-12v power supply – we were able to quickly and neatly add these quality lamps where needed. Installation of these does require basic soldering skills, but an installation diagram is provided with each pack to assist all modellers in equipping their layout.

The introduction of lighting to Twelve Trees Junction's town scene and station has changed the look of the layout, instantly adding more character and detail. The atmosphere it creates is excellent and the speed with which the Just-Plug lighting system can be connected up is impressive.

The step by step guide with this feature explains how we went about the installation. ∎

USEFUL LINKS	
Woodland Scenics	www.bachmann.co.uk
DCC Concepts Lamps	www.gaugemasterretail.com

SKILLS GUIDE: LAYOUT CONSTRUCTION

LIGHTING

STEP BY STEP: USING WOODLAND SCENICS' JUST-PLUG LIGHTING SYSTEM

1 The Just-Plug lighting system from Woodland Scenics encompasses all the parts you could need to install building lights – and it all just plugs together too: no soldering is required. The range includes lighting hubs, expansion hubs, stick on LED and nano LED lights in a variety of light colours, a light block kit, window film, a tidy wire kit, connecting cables and a power supply.

2 The standard lighting hub has a single input for power and four outputs to connect Just-Plug system lights to. Four dimmer controls are provided allowing each output to be adjusted to suit particular applications.

3 Most layout lighting situations will need more than four outputs and the Expansion Hub is the answer to that. It has been designed with 'in' and 'out' power connections allowing multiple Expansion Hubs to be connected together. Four hubs can then be connected from the right-hand four outputs. The maximum number of lights which can be run from a single power supply is 50.

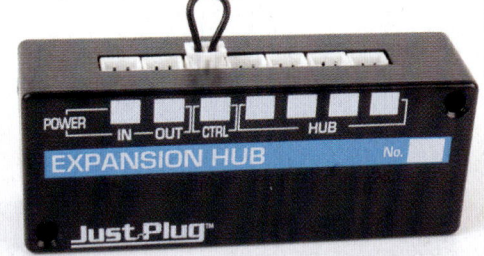

4 A standard connection has been designed for all Just-Plug components. All you have to do is join the cables in the right order by pushing the plugs into the correct sockets – it is that simple.

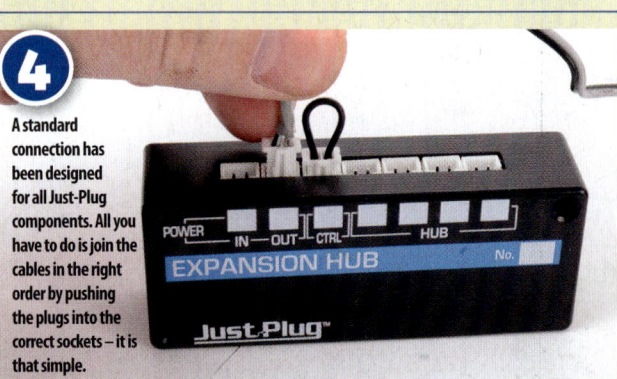

5 Illustrating a basic setup, from the left we have the mains power supply (which includes a built-in transformer), an Expansion Hub, a Light Hub and a single LED. This basic setup can be expanded to suit by connecting additional Expansion Hubs, Light Hubs and, finally, LEDs.

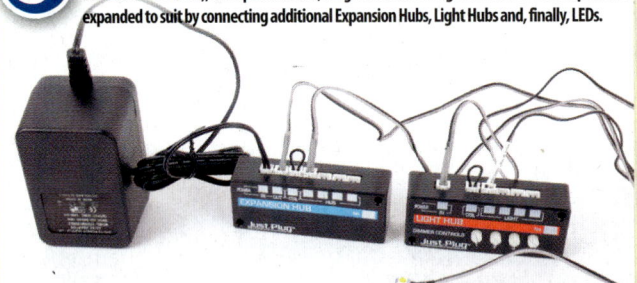

6 A lot of the work in this project is in preparing the buildings for interior lighting. By their very nature resin buildings leak light but Woodland Scenics has developed products to stop this problem. The Light Block kit contains a black rubber based paint and two rolls of black sealant. Painting the inside of the building with the black paint is the first step – the black sealant will be used later.

7 Having blacked out the building interior, and allowed the paint to dry fully, the next step is to add an LED. With just this single Stick On LED, the lighting wasn't particularly effective, but Woodland Scenics has developed a Light Diffusing Kit which changes the appearance of the lighting altogether.

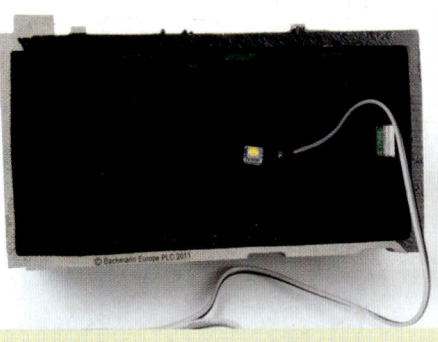

8 The Diffusing film from the Light Diffusing Kit (fixed in place with the contact adhesive) alters the performance of the light and means that a single Stick On LED can be used to illuminate the whole of this building.

9 To improve things further the Diffusing Kit also includes a Window Tint which has no effect on the quality of light from inside but stops light entering the building.

10 The Window Tint film needs to be immediately behind the window with the Diffusing Film behind that. Contact adhesive, carefully applied to avoid it appearing in the windows, was used to fix this layer in place.

LIGHTING

11 As well as the large Stick On LEDs, Woodland Scenics also produces packs of Nano LEDs – and these have huge potential. They are just 2mm in diameter and can be fitted into small spaces. To add extra lighting to this building we drilled a 2mm hole above the doors in the porch and then passed a Nano LED through from the inside.

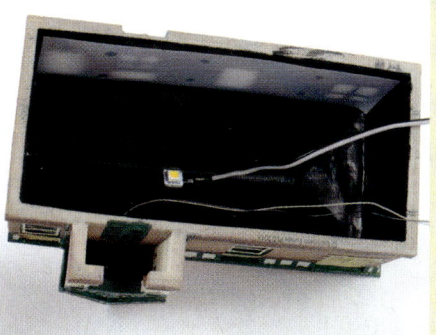

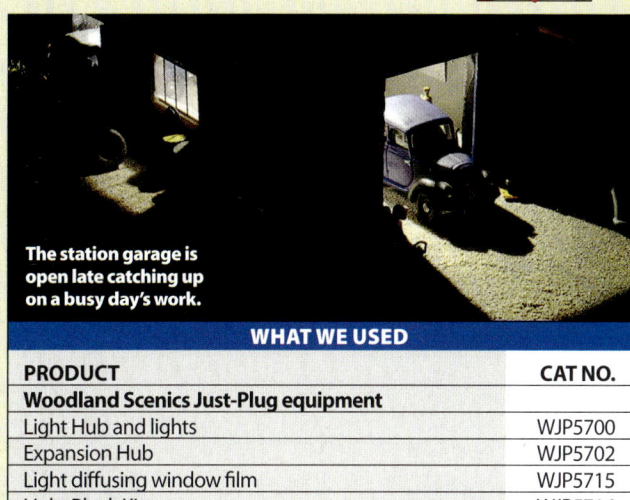

The station garage is open late catching up on a busy day's work.

12 Inside the blacked out roof it is difficult to see the Nano LED – the small spot of light is the giveaway. Once the room lights are turned down this addition makes a huge difference and is a perfect tool for lighting doorways. It could be used in many other locations too.

WHAT WE USED	
PRODUCT	**CAT NO.**
Woodland Scenics Just-Plug equipment	
Light Hub and lights	WJP5700
Expansion Hub	WJP5702
Light diffusing window film	WJP5715
Light Block Kit	WJP5716
Tidy Wire Kit	WJP5717
Stick on LEDS, warm white	WJP5740
Nano LEDS, warm white	WJP5743
Connecting cables	WJP5760
UK power supply	WJP5772
DCC Concepts swan neck lamps	
Swan neck lamp value pack, Southern Region green	GM867
Swan neck lamp value pack, soft black	GM866

13 To fit lights into the rest of the buildings for this project it is a simple case of repeating the steps above. Once you are ready to reposition the buildings an 8mm hole through the baseboard surface will accept the plug from each lamp.

14

Having drilled the hole and fed the wire through this building is ready to reinstate on the platform. Initially we temporarily positioned all the buildings to check for light leaks.

15 With all the buildings positioned loose in their locations and temporarily connected to the Light and Expansion Hubs and the lights turned on we were able to see how things were looking. It highlighted a couple of buildings where the Window Tint and Diffusing Film needed adjusting or redoing and also where light leaks were occurring from underneath buildings.

16 The station buildings were particularly prone to light leaks at their base. To prevent this we used the sealant – supplied in a rolled strip – from the Light Block Kit and pressed a length around the base of each building which was affected by light leaks.

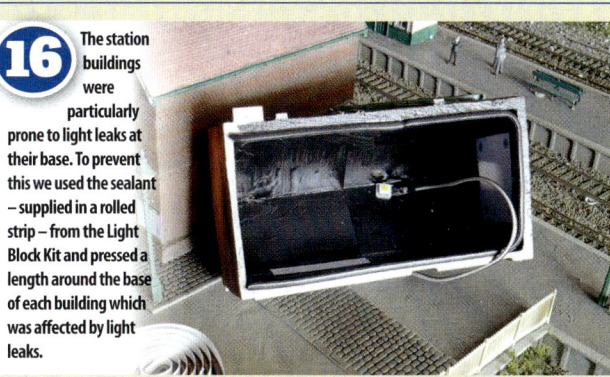

17

To fix the building in position we could have used just the sealant, but because this layout has to travel we opted to double up for safety and add contact adhesive around the building footings. It was then positioned on the layout and left to set – repeating the process for all other buildings.

18

We left the layout overnight for the buildings to set in place and then turned the baseboard on its side to allow final positioning of the wiring, Light and Expansion Hubs underneath.

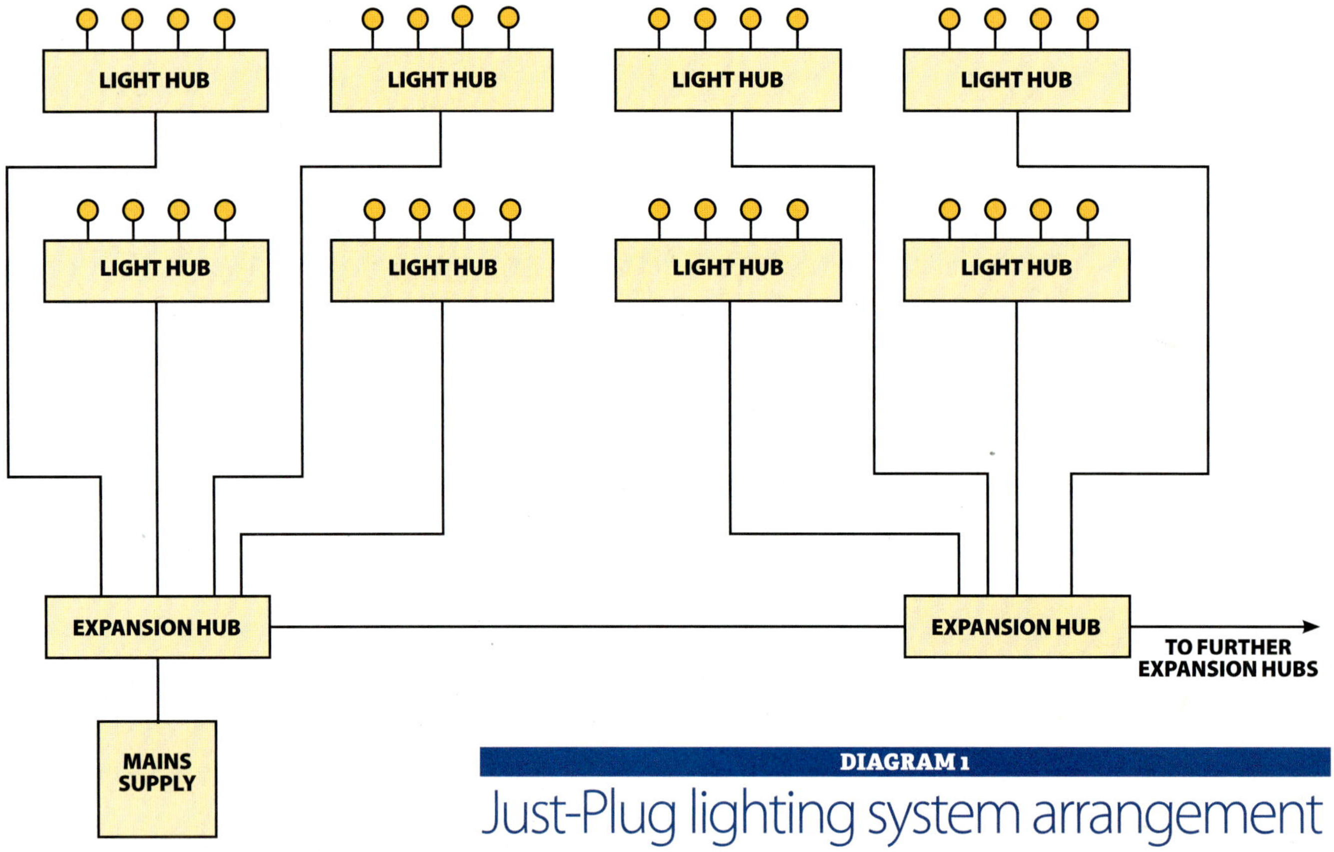

SKILLS GUIDE: LAYOUT CONSTRUCTION

LIGHTING

DIAGRAM 1
Just-Plug lighting system arrangement

STEP BY STEP: USING WOODLAND SCENICS' JUST-PLUG LIGHTING SYSTEM CONT...

SKILL LEVEL: Beginner – Intermediate – Advanced

19 First the Light Hubs were fixed underneath the baseboard in suitable positions to connect to the lights above using the supplied crosshead screws.

20 The wiring might look complex, but this is all simple repetition of the same circuit. This loose wiring will all need to be tidied up before it can be called complete – loose wires hanging from underneath will get damaged.

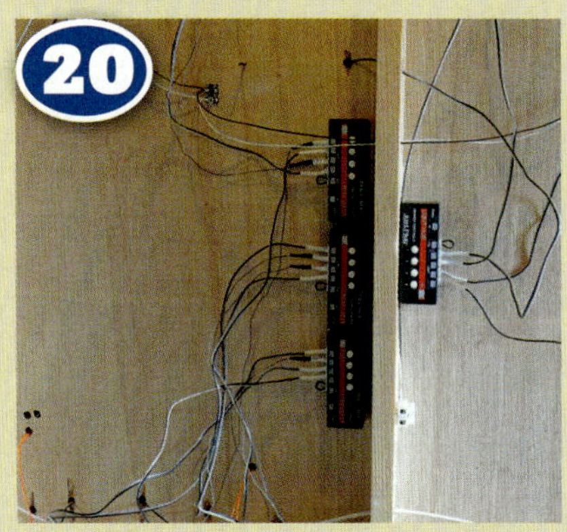

21 To allow all of the Light Hubs to be connected to the main power supply Expansion Hubs are needed. This project used two Expansion Hubs to feed six Light Hubs – each Expansion Hub can feed four Light Hubs. It is fixed to the baseboard using the screws provided.

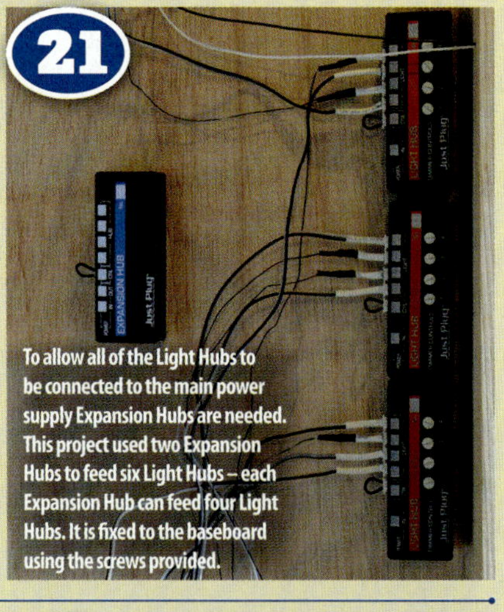

22 Using Connecting Cables the Expansion Hubs can be connected together and in turn the Light Hubs are connected to the outputs on the Expansion Hub – the process takes a matter of minutes – the only problem being what to do with the extra length of wire.

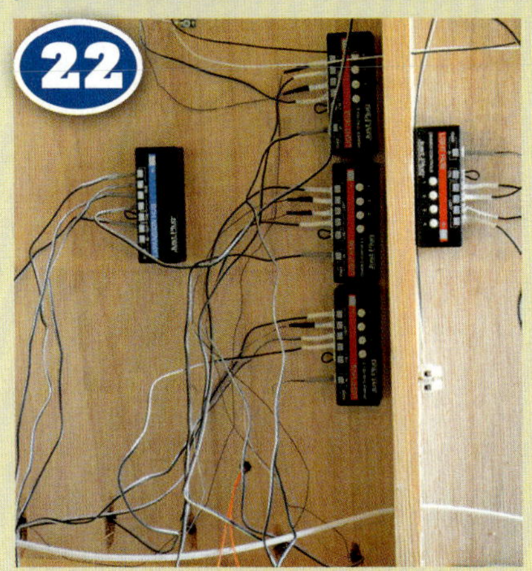

23 The Tidy Wire Kit produced as part of the Just-Plug system is an ideal and simple means of securing wires underneath the baseboard and grouping them together. Should you wish it also includes self adhesive labels which can be used to annotate the purpose of each wire.

24 With the wiring complete the installation was reconnected to the power supply and checked for operation. The brightness of each LED can be adjusted as required using the controls on each Light Hub.

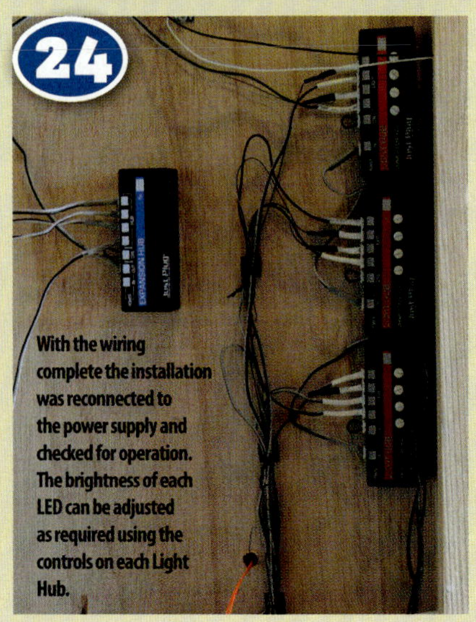

STEP BY STEP: WIRING DCC CONCEPTS STATION LAMPS

SKILL LEVEL: Intermediate

A To provide station and street lighting this layout is equipped with DCC Concepts Swan neck lamps. These are supplied in packs of three or six. Here we are using the Value Packs which contain six full height lamps with extensions, two wall mounted lamps and a pack of additional LEDs and circuit boards to operate both types of bulb.

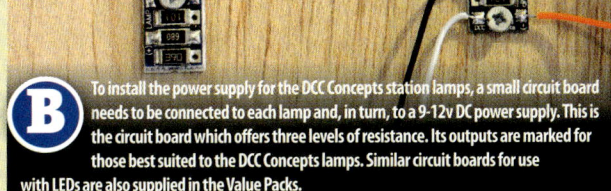

B To install the power supply for the DCC Concepts station lamps, a small circuit board needs to be connected to each lamp and, in turn, to a 9-12v DC power supply. This is the circuit board which offers three levels of resistance. Its outputs are marked for those best suited to the DCC Concepts lamps. Similar circuit boards for use with LEDs are also supplied in the Value Packs.

C The first step is to connect the wires from the lamp to the terminals on the circuit board. For simplicity and ease we extended the wires from this lamp with 7/0.2 multi-core wire. Polarity is not a problem so both wires are the same colour.

D To add a second lamp, a second circuit board was fixed underneath the baseboard and two orange wires from the lamp were soldered to the output terminals, as marked.

E The power supply terminals now need to be connected. As these are positive and negative we used black (positive) and white (negative) so that we could identify easily which wire was which in the installation.

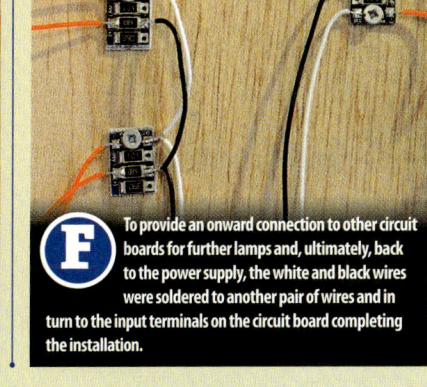

F To provide an onward connection to other circuit boards for further lamps and, ultimately, back to the power supply, the white and black wires were soldered to another pair of wires and in turn to the input terminals on the circuit board completing the installation.

A Just-Plug nano light lights the porch at Twelve Trees station.

SKILLS GUIDE: LAYOUT CONSTRUCTION

DETAILING *a railway*

Bringing a model railway to life means getting up close and personal with the world around the trains. **MARK CHIVERS** reveals *Hornby Magazine's* top tips to bring colour and life to any layout.

COUNTRY STATION

Detail is everywhere and replicating it in model form is highly rewarding. It takes a keen eye to get the features right as there is so much to see and include. At Shortley Bridge, a Thompson 'L1' 2-6-4T has just arrived with a rake of Gresley non-gangwayed carriages framed by a Hornby Skaledale footbridge.

Bringing life to the station is a guard from Dart Castings, Gaugemaster gas lamps in maroon, benches from the Hornby Skaledale range and Ratio spear fencing along the platform edges. Between the tracks, a section of rail, suitably rusted, has been left following track maintenance together with a trio of sleepers.

In front of the island platform, Woodland Scenics' fine leaf foliage blends the Scalescenes platform into its surroundings while on the left is an allotment produced with a range of Noch scenic accessories from its laser cut series as well as potted plants, tools and more. The fencing around the allotments is Ratio lineside fencing while the goods shed behind is a repainted Bachmann Scenecraft item which models the building at Shillingstone on the Somerset & Dorset Railway.

DETAILING

The goods shed at Shortley Bridge is served by a BT Models Karrier Bantam articulated lorry in BR crimson and cream colours. Its load is a Harburn Hamlet stone cast product. There are many suppliers of miniature pallets, including Scale Model Scenery. The cable drum is from Bachmann Scenecraft.

Period adverts always add colour and detail to a station scene including these by Sankey Scenics. Cut them out from the paper sheets and fix them to fencing or walls to suit your needs.

Gradient posts are a neat way of introducing a spot of detail to the lineside. Sankey Scenics produces packs of printed gradient signs which include suitable square section plastic strip to mount them on.

SKILLS GUIDE: LAYOUT CONSTRUCTION

DETAILING

DEPOT SCENES

Locomotive depots are both the simplest to get the appearance right on and the most complex to bring life to in miniature at the same time. Typically, a depot is well kept with little left lying around to allow workers safe passage around the site, but it is always tempting on a model railway to add clutter here there and everywhere.

However, at larger depots there is plenty of potential as shown here at the roundhouse scene built by *Hornby Magazine* in 2015. The main buildings are Scenecraft models sold exclusively by Kernow Model Rail Centre while the turntable is a Peco kit. These are available just as the basic kit while Peco produces an additional motorising kit.

The back of the depot buildings are kept clear as a passage for light commercial vehicles to reach the office. The Volkswagen pick-up is from Oxford Diecast while its plywood panel load is by Model Railway Scenery and is part of a builder's yard set. Meanwhile, the sidings have a temporary buffer stop in the form of a sleeper wrapped in chain. Coal sacks, Ratio plastic mouldings, have just been delivered and a member of staff is moving them to a safe location. In the siding where the Class 08 stands, spare wheelsets have been gathered from redundant carriages and painted in suitable rust colours to suggest that they have been standing outside for some time.

In the distance a couple of redundant pallets litter the ground together with a trio of sleepers stored from repairs to the siding previously. In the background you can see yard lights from Layouts 4U while the figures visible are both from the Dart Castings range.

A couple of hours spent painting details with a suitable array of muted browns and greys can add realistic detailing to a shed scene like this, without introduces any overstated pieces.

Lighting makes a big difference to a model railway and a wide range of products are available to suit any scene. Layouts 4U yard lamps, painted with Humbrol No. 29, illuminate the roundhouse and its turntable as a 'Hymek' is prepared for departure.

Buffer stops are integral to the end of every siding – and there is plenty of choice. Above left are the humble Peco rail built buffer stops (SL-40) which take seconds to assemble. Their appearance can be improved greatly with painting and weathering to take away the original plastic finish. Alternatively, for the best of the best, DCC Concepts produces superbly detailed scale bufferstops which are pre-fitted with a red lamp (above right).

SKILLS GUIDE: LAYOUT CONSTRUCTION

LIFE IN THE CITY

It's early in the morning at Grosvenor Square station and the staff are preparing for another busy day of arrivals and departures at this large Western Region terminus in the Midlands. Across the platform ends, hydraulic buffers by Peco are positioned to protect passengers should a train overrun while Ratio spear fencing makes sure that the passengers keep well away from the 'stops' as they walk onto the platforms.

Parcels and packages lay by the end of Platform 1 ready for loading into the next departing stopping train while on Platform 2 one of the porters has left a trolley of bagged mail. In front of the main station building the newspaper kiosk is ready for trade while, under the canopy, signage by Trackside Signs and period poster boards mean everyone knows where to go when they arrive to work in the city centre.

GWR benches, white metal kits by Dart Castings, line each platform illuminated under the Peco canopy by Gaugemaster Western Region coloured gas lamps. All it really needs now is a miniature population to go with the size of this seven-platform terminus. ■

Above: Trackside Signs produces a large collection of self-adhesive station signage and railway headed poster boards. These two are from a Western Region set to decorate the end of Grosvenor Square's station building.

DETAILING

Above: Sometimes it isn't just about the products you choose but how you use them. Here, Ratio's spear fencing gates pack has been used at the entrance to the platform with the gate left part open. Add to this newspapers by the kiosk by Dart Castings, a British Railways van and a pair of bicycles leaning against the fence and it all starts to suggest real life.

Platform numbers by Trackside Signs adorn the lamp while wicker baskets and milk churns by Hornby Skaledale join Model Scene luggage, suitably painted in brown.

USEFUL LINKS	
Bachmann/Woodland Scenics	www.bachmann.co.uk
BT Models	www.ayrey.co.uk
Dart Castings	www.dartcastings.co.uk
DCC Concepts	www.dccconcepts.com
Gaugemaster/Noch	www.gaugemasterretail.com
Harburn Hobbies	www.harburnhobbies.co.uk
Hornby	www.hornby.com
Kernow Model Rail Centre	www.kernowmodelrailcentre.com
Layouts 4U	www.layouts4u.net
Scale Model Scenery	www.scalemodelscenery.co.uk
Oxford Diecast	www.oxforddiecast.co.uk
Peco/Model Scene/Ratio	www.peco-uk.com
Sankey Scenics	www.sankeyscenics.co.uk
Trackside Signs	www.tracksidesigns.co.uk

SKILLS GUIDE: LAYOUT CONSTRUCTION

MAINTENANCE

Keeping the trains moving

You've built your layout and it's now ready to enjoy. **MIKE WILD** explains how to get the best from it with simple maintenance techniques and products which really make a difference.

↑ You can't beat a basic track rubber for keeping on top of track cleaning. Here we are using a well used Hornby R8087 rubber which has proved to be one of the best of its breed in our experience.

MAINTENANCE

Deluxe Materials Track Magic should be in every model railway toolbox. It cleans track, point blades and locomotive pick ups – in fact, it can clean any metal surface for consistent power collection. We wouldn't be without it!

EVERY RAILWAY NEEDS maintenance to keep it in perfect running order all the way down from the full-size railway to the smallest models. Keeping on top of track cleaning and locomotive servicing will result in a layout which is always a pleasure to operate. Leaving it to an annual clean would result in quite the opposite.

At the heart of consistent operation is electrical continuity. This comes in the form of clean railheads, point blades and wheels on the locomotives, consistent contact between the pick-ups on locomotives and neatly installed wiring and smoothly laid track.

There are many gadgets on the market to assist in model railway cleaning – some work just as described, but others are less effective than they might at first seem. For *Hornby Magazine's* layouts there is a simple cleaning tool kit: a Hornby track rubber, a Gaugemaster wheel cleaning brush and a bottle of Deluxe Materials Track Magic. It might not sound like much, but it really does the job.

Railhead treatments

So how do we use these products? The Hornby track rubber is used for general railhead cleaning. Other rubbers which we have used have tended to disintegrate during cleaning, which makes more of a mess than before cleaning in the first place. The Hornby track rubbers are stable and don't fall apart and make light work of cleaning everything from paint to general electrical dirt. We have two of these – one for heavy cleaning following painting and ballasting and one for the 'cleaner' job of general railhead cleaning.

Regular cleaning with a track rubber means we only need to carry out a light pass around the layout before a running session for our permanent office test track while the exhibition layouts will require a more thorough clean with a track rubber at the start of each event making sure that we don't miss any important areas. This is due to the periods in storage. Following this initial clean at a show, a quick whip round on the Saturday and Sunday morning sets the wheels in motion for an enjoyable operating session throughout the day.

An alternative which we have found both effective and useful is the Woodland Scenics Rail Tracker cleaning set. This consists of a plastic handle and a head which can host a variety of different cleaning pads. These work just as well as a handheld rubber but have the advantage »

Keeping a railway in the best condition starts with track cleaning – without this trains will stall on dirt accumulating on the railheads. Be prepared to vacuum your layout occasionally too to keep dust and fluff away from the trains. Here, we are using a Woodland Scenics Railtracker to clean the track through the station on Topley Dale.

SKILLS GUIDE: LAYOUT CONSTRUCTION

MAINTENANCE

A set of jewellers screwdrivers or a multi-driver device like this will be an essential tool for maintenance. The selection of screwdriver heads allows any locomotive body to be released quickly and with the right fitting

of a handle making it easier to manage the pads where access is more difficult due to baseboard width or the position of structures.

A third popular source of rail cleaning is a track cleaning wagon. A wide range of designs are available from Dapol's Track Cleaning wagon which can scrub, vacuum and polish rails. Other designs have cleaning cloths and fluids mounted on brass rollers to keep the railheads in the best possible condition for the next passing train. The advantage of these is that they need to be hauled around the layout so, with a little thought about routeing, they will never miss a spot. The downside is that they are a considerable outlay compared to a track rubber.

Deluxe Materials Track Magic is a toolbox essential for the *Hornby Magazine* team. It is a catch-all electrical cleaner (which we have even used to restore operation of a poor contact in a car light). It can be used to clean railheads using specially designed pads, but we keep it on hand for two purposes – cleaning between point blades and cleaning the back of locomotive wheels to maintain current collection through wiper pick-ups. It's an invaluable product which we highly recommend – just be aware that it will remove paint too, so use it carefully.

Locomotive maintenance

Maintenance extends beyond the track as locomotives need to be kept in premium condition to ensure they are always capable of running to the highest standards. As we have mentioned, Track Magic is a useful tool in cleaning pick-ups, but it can also be used for stubborn dirt on the wheels of locomotives in combination with a wheel cleaning brush.

For general cleaning of locomotive wheels, we use Gaugemaster's wheel cleaning brush. This is a plastic-cased pair of brass brushes which stands on top of the running rails to collect power which is then transferred

CLEANING PRODUCT CHOICES

PRODUCT	CAT NO.	PRICE
Gaugemaster wheel cleaning brush	GM60 ('OO'), GM59 ('N')	£25.00 (£20.00 – 'N')
Woodland Scenics Rail Tracker	TT4550 ('OO' and 'N')	£43.50
Deluxe Materials Track Magic	AC13	£11.75
Hornby track rubber	R8087	£3.30
Peco track rubber	PL-41	£4.95
Gaugemaster track rubber	GM27	£6.75
Dapol Track Cleaning wagon	B800	£90.00
Ten Commandments Track Cleaning Wagon	TCWOO ('OO'), TCWN ('N')	£40.00
CMX Clean Machine	'HO'/'OO'	Approx. £195.00
Sharge UK Track Cleaning wagon	'OO'	£105.00

USEFUL LINKS

Gaugemaster/Deluxe Materials	www.gaugemaster.com
Woodland Scenics	www.bachmann.co.uk
Hornby	www.hornby.com
Dapol	www.dapol.co.uk
Ten Commandments	www.tencommandmentsmodels.co.uk
CMX Clean Machine	www.dccconcepts.com
Sharge UK	www.model-trainstrack-cleaner.co.uk
Peco	www.peco-uk.com

MAINTENANCE

Just as important as maintaining the track is keeping locomotive wheels clean and fresh for consistent electrical connection with the track. We use a Gaugemaster GM60 rail mounted wheel cleaning brush to keep our locomotive wheels clean both at home and at exhibitions.

Beyond the basics of track rubbers there are a number of readily available track cleaning wagons. Dapol's track cleaning wagon can scrub, vacuum and polish the rails and includes its own motor to operate the vacuum. It still requires motive power to move it around a layout, as illustrated here by a pair of Class 20s.

Some of the track cleaning wagons on the market rely on fluid based cleaning, such as the Sharge UK Track Cleaning Unit. We tested this in 2017 and found it highly effective, once adjusted to suit our track layout, at removing dirt from rails. Like the Dapol cleaner it can be coupled to a locomotive for operation.

Proses produces a range of useful cradles to support locomotives during maintenance. This is one of its stands which is designed to support a model at an angle during repairs or maintenance.

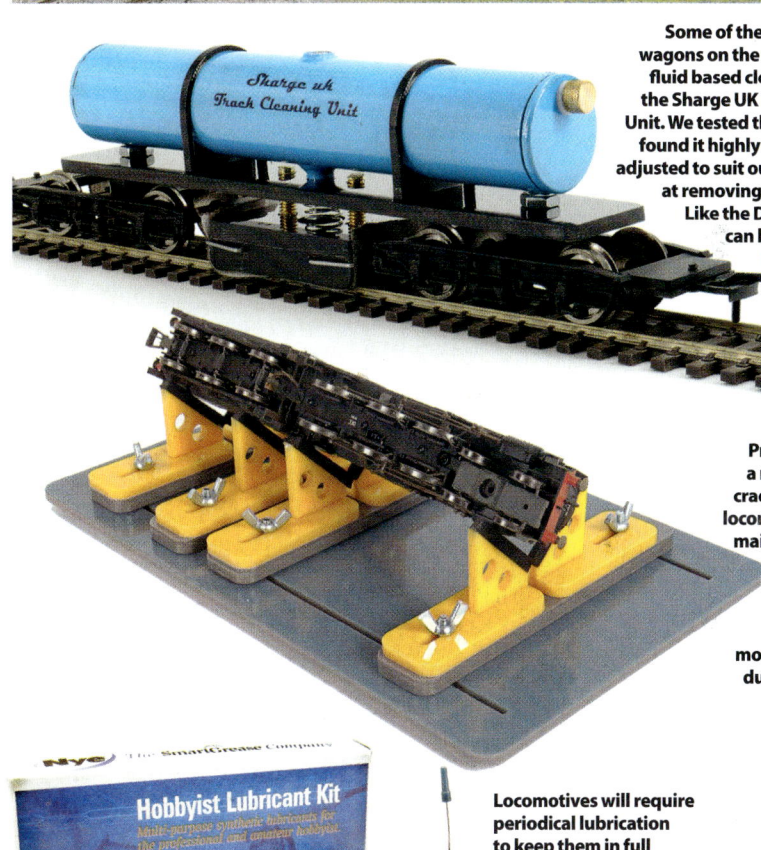

Locomotives will require periodical lubrication to keep them in full working order. Always apply specially designed hobby lubricants carefully – too much is as bad as none at all.

While not strictly maintenance, rerailing locomotives and rolling stock can be made easier with a rerailer. This is a powered device by Proses which allows locomotives to be driven straight onto the track.

through the brushes to a locomotive which is held on top. Light pressure ensures the brushes clean dirt from the wheels as they rotate, and this always restores service for a locomotive suffering from dirt. It's a simple process which takes no more than a minute or two to complete – and it is very worthwhile.

Beyond this, locomotives require occasional light oiling with a suitable model lubricant – don't be tempted to grab the nearest bottle of Castrol GTX – but always follow the instructions for oiling and be conservative in the quantity applied. Applying too much model oil is just as bad as having none.

Regular running

Keeping up with the basics of model railway maintenance will result in a great experience and a reliable layout which works time after time. It might seem at odds, but a regularly used layout will always fare better than one which is only switched on occasionally as the passing of trains assists in keeping the railway in the best order, especially if you follow a regular basic maintenance procedure.
Happy modelling! ■

YOUR ONLINE MODELLING

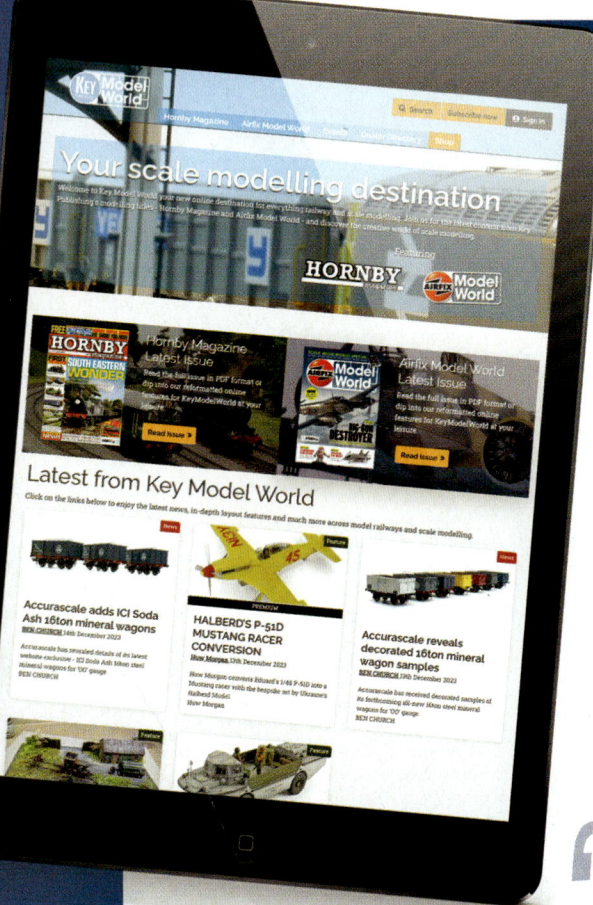

Unmissable modelling inspiration at your finger tips

"A modeller's paradise" — Christopher

"The key that unlocks the world of modelling!" — Graham

- ✓ Get all the **latest news** first
- ✓ **Exclusive** product and layout videos
- ✓ Fresh **inspiration**, tips and tricks every day
- ✓ More than **5,000 searchable** modelling articles
- ✓ Back issues of **Hornby Magazine**
- ✓ Full access to **Hornby Magazine** content
- ✓ All available on **any device** - *anywhere, anytime*

Visit:
www.keymod

SCALE DESTINATION

Featuring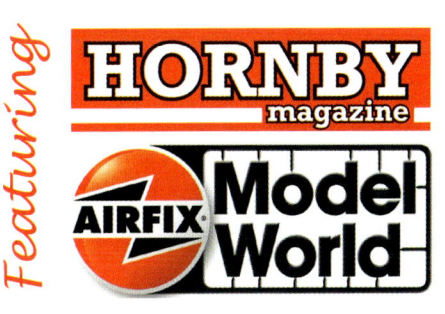

Exclusive video series!

NEW SERIES: Building a 'TT:120' model railway
A brand-new series is out now on Key Model World as the team embarks on its next project: a 'TT:120' scale layout. Join for this brand-new four-part series as we create Twelvemill Bridge. Don't miss it!

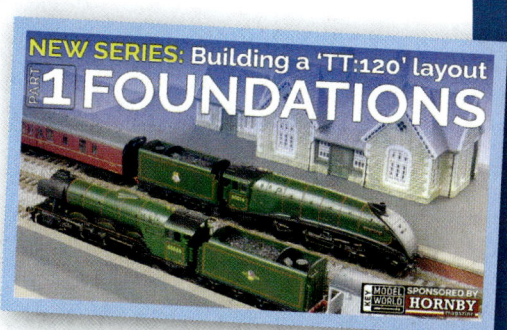

SERIES 5: 1960s Weathering
In our fifth series Mike Wild and Jonathan Newton show detailed techniques for weathering locomotives, carriages and wagons using powders, acrylics, washes and airbrushes. Watch the full series today.

SERIES 4: Flying Scotsman Centenary
2023 marks the 100th anniversary of the world's most famous steam locomotive – 60103 Flying Scotsman. We follow the locomotive during its visit to the Keighley and Worth Valley Railway in May 2023 to discover how the legend is kept alive.

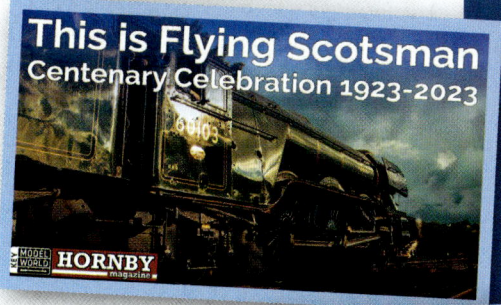

SERIES 3: Building a Diesel Depot
In our third video series we build a diesel depot using brand-new laser-cut kits from the Key Model World Shop collection in just 11ft x 2ft. Join the team as they show how you can do the same step by step.

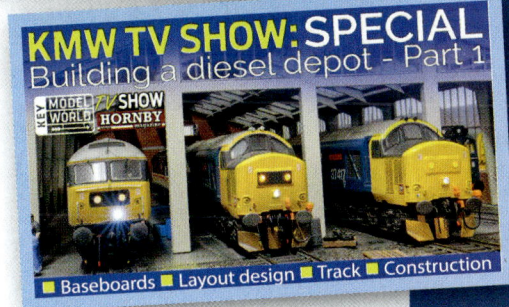

elworld.com

NEW SHOP
We have moved to a brand new bigger shop!

**Unit 9 Lake Road Aylesford
Kent ME20 7TQ**

We are open
Monday - Friday 10am - 4.30pm
Saturday 10am - 1pm

WE STOCK OVER 70 BRANDS INCLUDING

From G scale down to N Gauge

www.dreamsteam.co.uk
tel: 0800 022 4473 email: sales@dream-steam.com

EEZYLOADS

Quality mineral based model railway track ballast, model coal, wagon loads & scenic materials.

E: **sales@eezyloads.co.uk**
www.eezyloads.co.uk

Model Layout Services

Flat top baseboard (assembled)

Range of Laser Cut Baseboard kits - Flat top or Contour
Lightweight, quick & easy slot and tab assembly

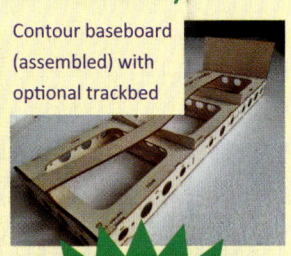

Contour baseboard (assembled) with optional trackbed

NEW Backscene and Lid
Bolt-on or build-in to our baseboards

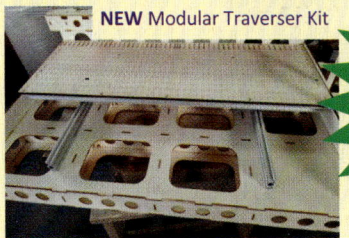

NEW Modular Traverser Kit

Start your layout on firm foundations

Flat top baseboard kits from £50

Shop at **www.modellayoutservices.co.uk**

chris@modellayoutservices.co.uk   07976 217624

A C Models
Tel: 02380 610100
www.acmodelseastleigh.co.uk

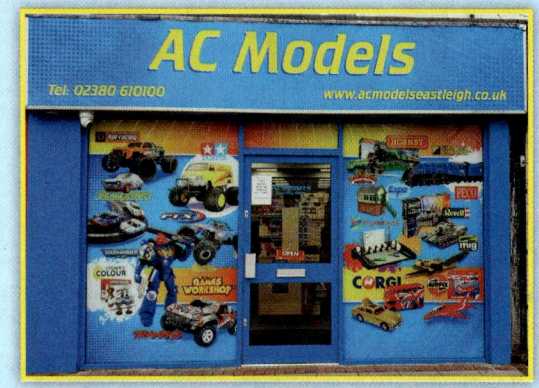

Two storeys of everything needed for your modelling needs. Radio control, Scalextric and games Workshop upstairs, Hornby, Corgi, plastic kits and lots more downstairs.

7/9 High Street, Eastleigh, Hants SO50 5LF
Email: **info@acmodelseastleigh.co.uk**
Ebay username: **acmodels2**
Open: **10am - 4pm** Closed: **Wednesdays & Sundays**